This Journal Belongs To:

_____

I Began This Journey On:

_____

I Finished This Journey On:

_____

A 90-DAY DISCIPLESHIP JOURNAL

Fan Into

Flames

"FOR THIS REASON, I AM REMINDING
YOU TO FAN INTO FLAMES THE GIFT OF
GOD THAT IS WITHIN YOU THROUGH THE
LAYING ON OF MY HANDS."
2 TIMOTHY 1:6

. . . .

Cover design: Brooklynn Spille of By The Brooke Design
Interior Hand-Lettering: Tiger Maddox, Claire Williams, and Emily Gray
Content and design: Tricia Patterson

. . . .

FOLLOW ON SOCIAL MEDIA
INSTAGRAM: @TLPAT
FACEBOOK: FACEBOOK.COM/TRICIAPATTERSONMINISTRIES
TWITTER: @TRISHLPATTERSON
WWW.TRICIAPATTERSON.COM

Tricia Patterson

MINISTRIES

Tricia Patterson Ministries exists to guide women into the presence of God as their roots grow down deeper into the soil of God's marvelous love through written resources and spoken word. We desire to *ignite wildfires* in hearts for Jesus Christ, we desire to *fan into flames* a passionate heart for God's Word and His people, we desire to *blaze trails* for His Eternal Kingdom, and we seek to make the name of Jesus Christ known by *any means possible.*

Fan Into Flames

JOURNAL TERMS & GUIDE

Spiritual Discipline:

Spiritual disciplines are activities, not attitudes. Disciplines are practices. Spiritual disciplines are things you do.
You read the Bible, pray, fast, worship, serve, confess and so forth.

The goal of practicing any discipline is not about doing as much as it is about being: being like Jesus, being with Jesus. The biblical way to grow in being more like Jesus is through the rightly motivated doing of the biblical, spiritual disciplines.

1 Timothy 4:7 says, "Discipline yourself for the purpose of godliness" (NASB).

The goal is godliness, but the biblical means to that is to discipline yourself by the power of the Holy Spirit rightly motivated.
We are to discipline ourselves for the purpose of godliness.

Don Whitney
https://www.desiringgod.org/interviews/what-are-spiritual-disciplines

The practical way of becoming more like Christ is by practicing biblical habits that foster authentic spiritual growth.

. . . .

Today's Passage:

Every day you will be given a specific passage to read in order to know exactly what to read. I know a major obstacle for many people in studying Scripture is not knowing where to start. Through the *Fan Into Flames* journal, you will read three different books of the Bible in their entirety: Philippians, James, and 1 John. I am confident you will thoroughly enjoy studying the Bible in this way.

. . . .

Observe | Head:

As you read each day's Scripture, I encourage you to work through the passage with the O, I, E Method.

The "O" stands for <u>Observe</u>. The observation section is the study section. During this stage, focus on the intellectual observations you can discover.

As you read each day's passage, take time to simply read and observe the context, key words and phrases, historical significance, and cross references to other passages in Scripture that are similar.

For those of you desiring to go even deeper, this is the section where you might use a commentary.

· ·

Internalize | Heart:

The next step is the "I", which stands for <u>Internalize</u>. This is the reflection section, connecting your heart to your head.

How will this passage change the way you think and feel? How does the truth in this passage impact your heart, your emotions, your attitude, your mind, your understanding? What does this passage teach you about yourself? What does it teach you about God?

· ·

Externalize | Hands:

Finally, you will go through the "E" step: Externalize. Here you will find a chance for application.

How will you take this passage beyond yourself? How will the truth in this Scripture impact the way you live? What can you do today to live out the truth in this Scripture? This is where we live out James 1:22 which says: *"Do not merely listen to the Word, and so deceive yourselves. Do what it says."*

. . . .

Prayer Posture:

In Biblical accounts of prayer, many postures are described. Abraham fell upon his face before God. *(Genesis 17:3, 17)* Moses prayed with his hands outstretched. *(Exodus 9:27-29)* King Solomon knelt in prayer. *(I Kings 8:54)* Jesus prayed looking up into heaven. *(Mark 6:41, John 11:41, and 17:1)*

Communication with God does not require a certain physical position, but postures do give expression to the attitudes of our hearts.

(https://iblp.org/questions/what-significance-using-different-postures-prayer)

I believe the posture of our hearts follows the posture of our physical bodies. As we kneel, lay prostrate, lift our hands, and more, we guide our hearts into a posture of worship.

. . . .

Prayer Focus:

Every day, you will find a "prayer focus" for the day to help center your mind in prayer. So often, we approach prayer feeling discombobulated, distracted, overwhelmed, or unsure of what to pray for. In contrast, prayer focuses give you clarity, direction, and confidence as you pray each day.

Using a different theme every day to guide you will not only make your prayer life more focused, but enable you to pray for a wide variety of things each week.

. . . .

Let's get started fanning into flames the gift of God in you!

Each week will include a Bible passage, prayer focuses & prompts, and a new spiritual discipline to build upon.
By the end of the <u>90 days</u>, you will read <u>3 complete books</u> of the Bible, and you will grow in <u>13 spiritual disciplines</u>!

This week's spiritual disciplines are Bible Study & Prayer.

As you study the Bible through the Fan Into Flames Journal, I encourage you to use the O, I, E method.
The "O" stands for <u>Observe</u>. As you read each day's passage, take time to simply read and observe the context, key words & phrases, historical significance, and cross references to other passages in Scripture that are similar.

The next step is the "I", which stands for Internalize. After observing what the passage is saying, I encourage you to internalize the passage. How will this passage change the way you think and feel? How does the truth in this passage impact your heart, your emotions, your attitude, your mind, your understanding?

Finally, you will go through the "E" step: Externalize. How will you take this passage beyond yourself?
How will the truth in this Scripture impact the way you live? What can you do today to live out the truth in this Scripture? This is where we live out James 1:22 which says:

"Do not merely listen to the Word, and so deceive yourselves.
Do what it says."

The other spiritual discipline for this week is the Discipline of Prayer. Each day, I provide a prayer focus for the day, along with a prayer posture. I believe the posture of our hearts follow the posture of our physical bodies. As we kneel, lay prostrate, lift our hands, and more, we lead our hearts to a worshipful posture.

Scripture Focus:
PHILIPPIANS 1

Spiritual Disciplines:
BIBLE STUDY
&
PRAYER

for me,
to live is
Christ
and to die
Gain

~PHILIPPIANS 1:21

Day 1	Date: 2/24/19

Time: 2:45   Place: Home

Today's Passage
PHILIPPIANS 1:1-6

OBSERVE :: HEAD

Study Section:

What are the key words, phrases, and
ideas I see in this passage?
What's the context and history?
What are the cross references?

Christ, live, die, gain

_____

_____

_____

_____

_____

INTERNALIZE :: HEART

Reflection Section:

How will this passage change the way I
think and feel?

_____

_____

_____

_____

_____

_____

_____

_____

_____

_____

_____

EXTERNALIZE :: HANDS

Application Section:

How will this passage change the way I
live?

_____

_____

_____

_____

_____

_____

_____

Key Verse from today:

Prayer Posture:
5 MINUTE PRAYER WALK

Prayer Focus:
MY COMMUNITY,
NATION, AND WORLD

_____

_____

_____

_____

_____

_____

Day 2   Date: 6:35am

Time 3/1/19   Place home

Today's Passage:
PHILIPPIANS 1:7-11

OBSERVE :: HEAD

Study Section:

What are the key words, phrases, and
ideas I see in this passage?
What's the context and history?
What are the cross references?

special favor, defending and
confirming the Good News.
growing in the knowledge and
understanding, fruit of your
salvation.

_____

_____

_____

_____

_____

INTERNALIZE :: HEART

Reflection Section:

How will this passage change the way I
think and feel?

_____

_____

_____

_____

_____

_____

_____

_____

_____

_____

EXTERNALIZE :: HANDS

Application Section:

How will this passage change the way I
live?

_____

_____

_____

_____

_____

_____

_____

_____

Key Verse from today:

Prayer Posture:
STAND WITH HANDS LIFTED HIGH

Prayer Focus:
MY FAMILY

_____

_____

_____

_____

_____

_____

_____

Day 3   Date: _____

Time: _____ Place: _____

Today's Passage:
PHILIPPIANS 1:12-19

OBSERVE :: HEAD

Study Section:

What are the key words, phrases, and
ideas I see in this passage?
What's the context and history?
What are the cross references?

_____

_____

_____

_____

_____

_____

_____

_____

_____

_____

INTERNALIZE :: HEART

Reflection Section:

How will this passage change the way I
think and feel?

_____

_____

_____

_____

_____

_____

_____

_____

_____

_____

EXTERNALIZE :: HANDS

Application Section:
How will this passage change the way I
live?

_____

_____

_____

_____

_____

_____

_____

Key Verse from today:

Prayer Posture:
KNEEL WITH HANDS OPEN TO HEAVEN

Prayer Focus:
MY FRIENDS

_____

_____

_____

_____

_____

_____

Day 4   Date: _____

Time _____ Place _____

Today's Passage
PHILIPPIANS 1:20-26

OBSERVE :: HEAD

Study Section:

What are the key words, phrases, and
ideas I see in this passage?
What's the context and history?
What are the cross references?

_____

_____

_____

_____

_____

_____

_____

_____

_____

_____

INTERNALIZE :: HEART

Reflection Section:

How will this passage change the way I think and feel?

_____

_____

_____

_____

_____

_____

_____

_____

_____

_____

EXTERNALIZE :: HANDS

Application Section:

How will this passage change the way I
live?

_____

_____

_____

_____

_____

_____

_____

Key Verse from today:

Prayer Posture:
PRAY OUT LOUD

Prayer Focus:
MY CURRENT CIRCUMSTANCES & TRIALS

_____

_____

_____

_____

_____

_____

Day 5   Date: _____

Time: _____ Place: _____

Today's Passage:
PHILIPPIANS 1:27-30

OBSERVE :: HEAD

Study Section:

What are the key words, phrases, and
ideas I see in this passage?
What's the context and history?
What are the cross references?

_____

_____

_____

_____

_____

_____

_____

_____

_____

_____

INTERNALIZE :: HEART

Reflection Section:

How will this passage change the way I
think and feel?

_____

_____

_____

_____

_____

_____

_____

_____

_____

_____

EXTERNALIZE :: HANDS

Application Section:

How will this passage change the way I live?

_____

_____

_____

_____

_____

_____

_____

Key Verse from today:

Prayer Posture:

SIT IN SILENCE & LISTEN TO GOD FOR 5
MINUTES

Prayer Focus:

MY GOALS, DREAMS, & DESIRES

_____

_____

_____

_____

_____

_____

Day 6   *Date:* _____

Time _____ *Place* _____

Today's Passage:
REREAD PHILIPPIANS 1

OBSERVE :: HEAD

Study Section:

Did you see anything new as you read
through the chapter for a 2nd time?

_____

_____

_____

_____

_____

_____

_____

_____

_____

_____

_____

_____

INTERNALIZE :: HEART

Reflection Section:

How will this passage change the way I
think and feel?

_____

_____

_____

_____

_____

_____

_____

_____

_____

_____

_____

EXTERNALIZE :: HANDS

Application Section:

How will this passage change the way I live?

_____

_____

_____

_____

_____

_____

_____

Key Verse from today:

Prayer Posture:

FIX YOUR GAZE ON HEAVEN & IMAGINE
STANDING AT THE THRONE OF GRACE

Prayer Focus:

THE SALVATION OF SOMEONE WHO IS
LOST

_____

_____

_____

_____

_____

_____

Day 7   Date: _____

Time: _____   Place: _____

Choose 1 verse to memorize from
PHILIPPIANS 1

I will memorize...

Prayer Posture:
KNEELING WHILE PRAYING OUT LOUD

Prayer Focus:

RECENT ANSWERED PRAYERS & REFLECTION ON GOD'S FAITHFULNESS

_____

_____

_____

_____

_____

_____

_____

_____

_____

_____

_____

_____

_____

_____

Welcome to Week 2!

I'm praying that the first week of this discipleship journal set your heart on fire for the Word of God, and I hope that your prayer life is actively being renewed and refreshed. Let's keep building on the spiritual disciplines you've already practiced!

This week, we will practice the Spiritual Discipline of Fasting. As you determine what you will fast this week, I want to explain a few things.

First, understand that fasting is voluntarily going without food — or any other regularly enjoyed, good gift from God — for the sake of some spiritual purpose.

Second, you should never fast a sin. For example: gossiping, lying, worrying, cheating. These are sins you should repent of, these are not things you should fast.

Third, choose something realistic and sacrificial. Don't choose something unmanageable, choose something realistic. On the other hand, don't take the easy way out. Be sure that you are sacrificing something for the sake of gaining more of Christ.

Some realistic & sacrificial options:
- One meal a day.
- Your favorite beverage. (Soft drinks, Starbucks, etc.)
- Social Media. (Facebook, Instagram, Snapchat)

We will begin the fast on the evening of <u>Day 8</u>, and we will complete the fast on the evening of <u>Day 14</u>. Choose wisely!

Scripture Focus:

PHILIPPIANS 2

Spiritual Disciplines:

BIBLE STUDY
PRAYER
& FASTING

»PHIL 2:5«

let this mind be in you ≫

which was in

≫ *Christ Jesus* ≪

Day 8   Date: _____

Time: _____ Place: _____

Today's Passage
PHILIPPIANS 2:1-4

OBSERVE :: HEAD

Study Section:

What are the key words, phrases, and
ideas I see in this passage?

_____

_____

_____

_____

_____

_____

_____

_____

_____

INTERNALIZE :: HEART

Reflection Section:

How will this passage change the way I
think and feel?

_____

_____

_____

_____

_____

_____

_____

_____

EXTERNALIZE :: HANDS

Application Section:

How will this passage change the way I live?

_____

_____

_____

_____

_____

_____

_____

Key Verse from today:

What will you be fasting this week?

I will be fasting...

Prayer Posture:
5 MINUTE PRAYER WALK

Prayer Focus:
MY COMMUNITY,
NATION, AND WORLD

_____

_____

_____

_____

_____

_____

Day 9   Date: _____

Time: _____   Place: _____

Today's Passage
PHILIPPIANS 2:5-11

OBSERVE :: HEAD

Study Section:

What are the key words, phrases, and ideas I see in this passage?

_____

_____

_____

_____

_____

_____

_____

_____

_____

_____

_____

_____

INTERNALIZE :: HEART

Reflection Section:

How will this passage change the way I
think and feel?

_____

_____

_____

_____

_____

_____

_____

_____

_____

_____

EXTERNALIZE :: HANDS

Application Section:

How will this passage change the way I
live?

_____

_____

_____

_____

_____

_____

_____

Key Verse from today:

Fast Update

As you fast, spend quality time with God in prayer. Each time you are hungry or long for the thing that you have given up, turn your heart to God and relate to Him instead. Remind yourself that your real hunger is to know God and depend on Him to sustain and satisfy you.

Today's fasting struggles:

Today's fasting victories:

Prayer Posture:

PRAY WHILE LYING PROSTRATE ON THE
FLOOR

Prayer Focus:

MY FAMILY

_____

_____

_____

_____

_____

_____

_____

_____

_____

Day 10　　　　　Date: _____

Time: _____　Place: _____

Today's Passage
PHILIPPIANS 2:12-18

<u>OBSERVE :: HEAD</u>

Study Section:

What are the key words, phrases, and
ideas I see in this passage?

_____

_____

_____

_____

_____

_____

_____

_____

_____

_____

_____

_____

INTERNALIZE :: HEART

Reflection Section:

How will this passage change the way I
think and feel?

_____

_____

_____

_____

_____

_____

_____

_____

_____

_____

_____

EXTERNALIZE :: HANDS

Application Section:

How will this passage change the way I
live?

_____

_____

_____

_____

_____

_____

_____

Key Verse from today:

Fast Update

Today's fasting struggles:

Today's fasting victories:

Prayer Posture:

KNEEL WITH HANDS OPEN TO HEAVEN

Prayer Focus:

MY FRIENDS

_____

_____

_____

_____

_____

_____

_____

_____

_____

_____

| Day 11 | Date: _____ |

Time: _____ Place: _____

Today's Passage:
PHILIPPIANS 2:19-24

OBSERVE :: HEAD

Study Section:

What are the key words, phrases, and ideas I see in this passage?

_____

_____

_____

_____

_____

_____

_____

_____

_____

_____

_____

_____

INTERNALIZE :: HEART

Reflection Section:

How will this passage change the way I
think and feel?

_____

_____

_____

_____

_____

_____

_____

_____

_____

_____

EXTERNALIZE :: HANDS

Application Section:

How will this passage change the way I
live?

_____

_____

_____

_____

_____

_____

_____

Key Verse from today:

Fast Update

Today's fasting struggles:

Today's fasting victories:

Prayer Posture:
STAND WITH HANDS LIFTED HIGH

Prayer Focus:
MY CURRENT CIRCUMSTANCES & TRIALS

_____

_____

_____

_____

_____

_____

_____

_____

_____

Day 12

Date: _____

Time: _____ Place: _____

Today's Passage.
PHILIPPIANS 2:25-30

OBSERVE :: HEAD

Study Section:

What are the key words, phrases, and ideas I see in this passage?

_____

_____

_____

_____

_____

_____

_____

_____

_____

_____

_____

_____

INTERNALIZE :: HEART

Reflection Section:

How will this passage change the way I
think and feel?

_____

_____

_____

_____

_____

_____

_____

_____

_____

_____

EXTERNALIZE :: HANDS

Application Section:

How will this passage change the way I
live?

_____

_____

_____

_____

_____

_____

_____

Key Verse from today:

Fast Update

Today's fasting struggles:

Today's fasting victories:

Prayer Posture:

SIT IN SILENCE & LISTEN TO GOD FOR 5 MINUTES

Prayer Focus:

MY GOALS, DREAMS, & DESIRES

_____

_____

_____

_____

_____

_____

_____

_____

_____

_____

_____

Day 13	Date: _____

Time: _____ Place: _____

Today's Passage:
REREAD PHILIPPIANS 2

<u>OBSERVE :: HEAD</u>

Study Section:

Did you see anything new as you read
through the chapter for a 2nd time?

_____

_____

_____

_____

_____

_____

_____

_____

_____

_____

_____

_____

INTERNALIZE :: HEART

Reflection Section:

How will this passage change the way I think and feel?

_____

_____

_____

_____

_____

_____

_____

_____

_____

_____

EXTERNALIZE :: HANDS

Application Section:

How will this passage change the way I
live?

_____

_____

_____

_____

_____

_____

_____

Key Verse from today:

Fast Update

Today's fasting struggles:

Today's fasting victories:

Prayer Posture:

FIX YOUR GAZE ON HEAVEN & IMAGINE
STANDING AT THE THRONE OF GRACE

Prayer Focus:

THE SALVATION OF SOMEONE WHO IS
LOST

_____

_____

_____

_____

_____

_____

_____

_____

_____

Day 14   Date: _____

Time: _____ Place: _____

Choose 1 verse to memorize from
PHILIPPIANS 2

I will memorize...

Prayer Posture:
KNEELING WHILE PRAYING OUT LOUD

Prayer Focus:
RECENT ANSWERED PRAYERS

_____

_____

_____

_____

How was this week's fast?
What did God teach you?

This week, we will be entering into very focused times of worship.

I view worship as a way of getting our spiritual blood pumping. For me, worship is one of the ways I align my heart to the Father's. Worship elevates my mind and emotions to a heavenly place.

Louie Giglio says, "Worship is giving God His breath back."

As we enter into this week, concentrating on the Discipline of Worship, we will primarily practice worship through song. Each day, I encourage you to focus on one specific response towards God in worship (i.e. praise, humility, surrender, etc.)

I encourage you to find a song that correlates with that specific response. For example, a song of praise might be: "Shout to the Lord."

As you listen to each song, direct your mind towards God, and share in the journal your heart's response.

Scripture Focus:

PHILIPPIANS 3

Spiritual Disciplines:

BIBLE STUDY
PRAYER
FASTING
& WORSHIP

Forgetting what
is behind and
straining toward the
goal to win the
prize for which
God has called
me heavenward
in Christ
Jesus
— PHILIPPIANS
3:13-14

Day 15	Date: _____

Time: _____ Place: _____

Today's Passage:
PHILIPPIANS 3:1-3

OBSERVE :: HEAD

Study Section:

What are the key words, phrases, and ideas I see in this passage?

_____

_____

_____

_____

_____

_____

_____

_____

_____

_____

INTERNALIZE :: HEART

Reflection Section:

How will this passage change the way I
think and feel?

_____

_____

_____

_____

_____

_____

_____

_____

_____

EXTERNALIZE :: HANDS

Application Section:

How will this passage change the way I live?

_____

_____

_____

_____

_____

_____

_____

Key Verse from today:

Today in worship, focus on praise...

Song(s):

Heart Response:

Prayer Posture:
5 MINUTE PRAYER WALK

Prayer Focus:
MY COMMUNITY,
NATION, AND WORLD

_____

_____

_____

_____

_____

_____

Day 16   Date: _____

Time: _____ Place: _____

Today's Passage:
PHILIPPIANS 3:4-6

OBSERVE :: HEAD

Study Section:

What are the key words, phrases, and
ideas I see in this passage?

_____

_____

_____

_____

_____

_____

_____

_____

_____

_____

INTERNALIZE :: HEART

Reflection Section:

How will this passage change the way I think and feel?

_____

_____

_____

_____

_____

_____

_____

_____

_____

EXTERNALIZE :: HANDS

Application Section:

How will this passage change the way I live?

Key Verse from today:

Today in worship, focus on humility...

Song(s):

Heart Response:

Prayer Posture:
STAND WITH HANDS LIFTED HIGH

Prayer Focus:
MY FAMILY

_____

_____

_____

_____

_____

_____

Day 17   Date: _____

Time: _____ Place: _____

Today's Passage:
PHILIPPIANS 3:7-11

OBSERVE :: HEAD

Study Section:

What are the key words, phrases, and
ideas I see in this passage?

_____

_____

_____

_____

_____

_____

_____

_____

_____

_____

INTERNALIZE :: HEART

Reflection Section:

How will this passage change the way I
think and feel?

_____

_____

_____

_____

_____

_____

_____

_____

_____

EXTERNALIZE :: HANDS

Application Section:

How will this passage change the way I live?

Key Verse from today:

Today in worship, focus on surrender...

Song(s):

Heart Response:

Prayer Posture:
FIX YOUR GAZE ON HEAVEN & IMAGINE
STANDING AT THE THRONE OF GRACE

Prayer Focus:
MY FRIENDS

_____

_____

_____

_____

_____

Day 18   Date: _____

Time: _____   Place: _____

Today's Passage
PHILIPPIANS 3:12-16

OBSERVE :: HEAD

Study Section:

What are the key words, phrases, and
ideas I see in this passage?

_____

_____

_____

_____

_____

_____

_____

_____

_____

_____

INTERNALIZE :: HEART

Reflection Section:

How will this passage change the way I think and feel?

_____

_____

_____

_____

_____

_____

_____

EXTERNALIZE :: HANDS

Application Section:

How will this passage change the way I live?

_____

_____

_____

_____

_____

_____

_____

Key Verse from today:

Today in worship, focus on hope...

Song(s):

Heart Response:

Prayer Posture:

KNEEL WITH HANDS OPEN TO HEAVEN

Prayer Focus:

MY CURRENT CIRCUMSTANCES & TRIALS

_____

_____

_____

_____

_____

_____

Day 19   Date: _____

Time: _____ Place: _____

Today's Passage

PHILIPPIANS 3:17-21

OBSERVE :: HEAD

Study Section:

What are the key words, phrases, and ideas I see in this passage?

_____

_____

_____

_____

_____

_____

_____

_____

_____

INTERNALIZE :: HEART

> Reflection Section:
>
> How will this passage change the way I
> think and feel?

_____

_____

_____

_____

_____

_____

_____

_____

EXTERNALIZE :: HANDS

<u>Application Section:</u>

How will this passage change the way I live?

_____

_____

_____

_____

_____

_____

_____

_____

Key Verse from today:

Today in worship, focus on victory...

Song(s):

Heart Response:

Prayer Posture:
PRAY WHILE LYING PROSTRATE ON THE
FLOOR

Prayer Focus:
MY GOALS, DREAMS, & DESIRES

_____

_____

_____

_____

_____

_____

Day 20   Date: _____

Time: _____ Place: _____

Today's Passage:
REREAD PHILIPPIANS 3

OBSERVE :: HEAD

Study Section:

Did you see anything new as you read
through the chapter for a 2nd time?

_____

_____

_____

_____

_____

_____

_____

_____

_____

_____

_____

INTERNALIZE :: HEART

Reflection Section:

How will this passage change the way I
think and feel?

_____

_____

_____

_____

_____

_____

_____

EXTERNALIZE :: HANDS

Application Section:

How will this passage change the way I live?

_____

_____

_____

_____

_____

_____

_____

Key Verse from today:

Today in worship, focus on obedience...

Song(s):

Heart Response:

Prayer Posture:

SIT IN SILENCE & LISTEN TO GOD FOR 5 MINUTES

Prayer Focus:

THE SALVATION OF SOMEONE WHO IS LOST

_____

_____

_____

_____

_____

Day 21   Date: _____

Time: _____ Place: _____

Choose 1 verse to memorize from
PHILIPPIANS 3

I will memorize...

Prayer Posture:
KNEELING WHILE PRAYING OUT LOUD

Prayer Focus:

RECENT ANSWERED PRAYERS

_____

_____

_____

_____

What did God teach you during this focused week of worship?

This week, we will focus on the spiritual Discipline of Meditation. Many misinterpret what meditation truly means. Christian meditation is not like the "New Age" meditation you may have heard of. Biblical meditation means to focus, concentrate, and ponder on the truth of God's Word to gain closeness and intimacy with the One True God. The goal of Christian meditation is to internalize and personalize the Scripture so that its truth can affect how we think, our attitudes, and how we live, our actions.

Throughout Scripture, believers are encouraged to meditate. This is a discipline we often neglect in our culture today because of the many distractions we are faced with on a daily basis.

"Let the words of my mouth and the meditation of my heart be acceptable in your sight, O Lord, my rock and my redeemer."
Psalm 19:14

Scripture Focus:

PHILIPPIANS 4

Spiritual Disciplines:

BIBLE STUDY,
PRAYER
FASTING
WORSHIP
& MEDITATION

BRETHREN *Whatever* *things* *are* TRUE, NOBLE, JUST, PURE, LOVELY, OF GOOD REPORT & *if* *there* *is* *any* VIRTUE, *anything* PRAISEWORTHY MEDITATE ON THESE THINGS

PHILIPPIANS 4:8

Day 22   Date: _____

Time _____   Place _____

Today's Passage
PHILIPPIANS 4:1-3

OBSERVE :: HEAD

Study Section:

What are the key words, phrases, and
ideas I see in this passage?

_____

_____

_____

_____

_____

_____

_____

INTERNALIZE :: HEART

Reflection Section:

How will this passage change the way I
think and feel?

_____

_____

_____

_____

_____

_____

_____

_____

_____

_____

_____

EXTERNALIZE :: HANDS

Application Section:

How will this passage change the way I live?

_____

_____

_____

_____

_____

_____

_____

Key Verse from today:

Meditate

Take 5 minutes: Focus, ponder, & reflect
upon Christ's love for you.
Jot down your thoughts.

Prayer Posture:

FIX YOUR GAZE ON HEAVEN & IMAGINE
STANDING AT THE THRONE OF GRACE

Prayer Focus:

MY COMMUNITY,
NATION, AND WORLD

_____

_____

_____

_____

_____

_____

_____

_____

_____

_____

_____

Day 23   Date: _____

Time: _____ Place: _____

Today's Passage:
PHILIPPIANS 4:4-7

OBSERVE :: HEAD

Study Section:

What are the key words, phrases, and
ideas I see in this passage?

_____

_____

_____

_____

_____

_____

_____

_____

_____

INTERNALIZE :: HEART

Reflection Section:

How will this passage change the way I
think and feel?

_____

_____

_____

_____

_____

_____

_____

_____

_____

EXTERNALIZE :: HANDS

Application Section:

How will this passage change the way I
live?

_____

_____

_____

_____

_____

_____

_____

Key Verse from today:

Meditate

Take 5 minutes: Focus, ponder, & reflect
on a verse from today's passage.
Jot down your thoughts.

Prayer Posture:

STAND WITH HANDS LIFTED HIGH

Prayer Focus:

MY FAMILY

_____

_____

_____

_____

_____

_____

_____

_____

_____

_____

Day 24   Date: _____

Time: _____   Place: _____

Today's Passage:
PHILIPPIANS 4:8-9

OBSERVE :: HEAD

Study Section:

What are the key words, phrases, and
ideas I see in this passage?

_____

_____

_____

_____

_____

_____

_____

_____

_____

INTERNALIZE :: HEART

Reflection Section:

How will this passage change the way I
think and feel?

_____

_____

_____

_____

_____

_____

_____

_____

_____

EXTERNALIZE :: HANDS

Application Section:

How will this passage change the way I
live?

_____

_____

_____

_____

_____

_____

_____

_____

Key Verse from today:

Meditate

Contemplate the meaning of
Philippians 4:8-9 for 5 minutes.
Jot down your thoughts.

Prayer Posture:

PRAY WHILE LYING PROSTRATE ON THE
FLOOR

Prayer Focus:

MY FRIENDS

_____

_____

_____

_____

_____

_____

_____

_____

_____

_____

Day 25   Date: _____

Time: _____ Place: _____

Today's Passage:
PHILIPPIANS 4:10-14

OBSERVE :: HEAD

Study Section:

What are the key words, phrases, and
ideas I see in this passage?

_____

_____

_____

_____

_____

_____

_____

_____

_____

_____

_____

INTERNALIZE :: HEART

Reflection Section:

How will this passage change the way I think and feel?

_____

_____

_____

_____

_____

_____

_____

EXTERNALIZE :: HANDS

Application Section:

How will this passage change the way I live?

_____

_____

_____

_____

_____

_____

_____

Key Verse from today:

Meditate

Choose one worship song to listen to and meditate upon the meaning of the words.
Share your thoughts below.

Prayer Posture:

5 MINUTE PRAYER WALK

Prayer Focus:

MY CURRENT CIRCUMSTANCES & TRIALS

_____

_____

_____

_____

_____

_____

_____

_____

_____

_____

Day 26	Date: _____

Time: _____ Place: _____

Today's Passage
PHILIPPIANS 4:15-23

OBSERVE :: HEAD

Study Section:

What are the key words, phrases, and ideas I see in this passage?

_____

_____

_____

_____

_____

_____

_____

_____

_____

_____

INTERNALIZE :: HEART

Reflection Section:

How will this passage change the way I
think and feel?

_____

_____

_____

_____

_____

_____

_____

_____

EXTERNALIZE :: HANDS

Application Section:

How will this passage change the way I
live?

_____

_____

_____

_____

_____

_____

_____

_____

Key Verse from today:

Meditate

Pray the following:
"Search me, God, and know my heart;
test me and know my anxious thoughts."
(Psalm 139:23)
Ask God to expose any wrong thoughts
or attitudes in your heart.
Share below what God revealed to you.

Prayer Posture:

KNEEL WITH HANDS OPEN TO HEAVEN

Prayer Focus:

MY GOALS, DREAMS, & DESIRES

_____

_____

_____

_____

_____

_____

_____

_____

_____

_____

Day 27   Date: _____

Time: _____ Place: _____

Today's Passage:
REREAD PHILIPPIANS 4

OBSERVE :: HEAD

Study Section:

Did you see anything new as you read
through the chapter for a 2nd time?

_____

_____

_____

_____

_____

_____

_____

_____

_____

_____

INTERNALIZE :: HEART

Reflection Section:

How will this passage change the way I think and feel?

_____

_____

_____

_____

_____

_____

_____

_____

_____

EXTERNALIZE :: HANDS

Application Section:

How will this passage change the way I live?

_____

_____

_____

_____

_____

_____

_____

_____

Key Verse from today:

Meditate

Reflect upon Philippians 4 for 5 minutes. Which verses spoke to you most deeply and why?

Prayer Posture:

KNEELING WHILE PRAYING OUT LOUD

Prayer Focus:

THE SALVATION OF SOMEONE WHO IS
LOST

_____

_____

_____

_____

_____

_____

_____

_____

_____

Day 28   Date: _____

Time: _____ Place: _____

Choose 1 verse to memorize from
PHILIPPIANS 4

I will memorize...

Prayer Posture:
SIT IN SILENCE & LISTEN TO GOD FOR 5
MINUTES

Prayer Focus:

RECENT ANSWERED PRAYERS

_____

_____

_____

_____

What did God teach you during this focused week of meditation?

Welcome to Week 5!

This week's new spiritual discipline is the Discipline of Silence & Solitude. This is a spiritual discipline that has fallen to the wayside in many ways because of the busy & noisy nature of our culture. I am positive that you will experience rest, rejuvenation, and fullness of heart through this discipline.

Many of us feel very uncomfortable when we are alone, but God is calling us from loneliness to solitude of soul. From the noisiness of jumbled emotion to the silence of a content heart. Join me in the journey towards silence & solitude.

"We can cultivate an inner solitude and silence that sets us free from loneliness and fear. Loneliness is inner emptiness. Solitude is inner fulfillment."
– Richard Foster

Scripture Focus:

JAMES 1

Spiritual Disciplines:

BIBLE STUDY
PRAYER
FASTING
WORSHIP
MEDITATION
& SILENCE + SOLITUDE

count it all JOY my brothers and sisters when you meet trials of various kinds

— James 1:2

Day 29   Date: _____

Time: _____ Place: _____

Today's Passage
JAMES 1:1-4

OBSERVE :: HEAD

Study Section:

What are the key words, phrases, and ideas I see in this passage?

_____

_____

_____

_____

_____

_____

_____

_____

_____

INTERNALIZE :: HEART

Reflection Section:

How will this passage change the way I
think and feel?

_____

_____

_____

_____

_____

_____

_____

_____

EXTERNALIZE :: HANDS

Application Section:

How will this passage change the way I live?

_____

_____

_____

_____

_____

_____

_____

Key Verse from today:

Silence & Solitude

Get alone. Get quiet.
Turn your phone off. Take 10 minutes.
Choose one verse from today's
passage to meditate upon.
Share your thoughts below.

Prayer Posture:

STAND WITH HANDS LIFTED HIGH

Prayer Focus:

MY COMMUNITY,
NATION, AND WORLD

_____

_____

_____

_____

_____

_____

_____

_____

_____

Day 30   Date: _____

Time: _____ Place: _____

Today's Passage:
JAMES 1:5-8

OBSERVE :: HEAD

Study Section:

What are the key words, phrases, and
ideas I see in this passage?

_____

_____

_____

_____

_____

_____

_____

_____

_____

INTERNALIZE :: HEART

Reflection Section:

How will this passage change the way I
think and feel?

_____

_____

_____

_____

_____

_____

_____

_____

_____

EXTERNALIZE :: HANDS

Application Section:

How will this passage change the way I live?

_____

_____

_____

_____

_____

_____

_____

_____

Key Verse from today:

Silence & Solitude

Find a quiet spot to get alone.
(i.e. a spot in a park, a church
sanctuary, or even a closet)
Take 10 minutes to stay silent and
listen for God to speak to you.
Share below any ways God stirs your
heart.

Prayer Posture:

KNEEL WITH HANDS OPEN TO HEAVEN

Prayer Focus:

MY FAMILY

_____

_____

_____

_____

_____

_____

_____

_____

_____

_____

_____

Day 31   Date: _____

Time: _____ Place: _____

Today's Passage:
JAMES 1:9-11

OBSERVE :: HEAD

Study Section:

What are the key words, phrases, and
ideas I see in this passage?

_____

_____

_____

_____

_____

_____

_____

_____

_____

INTERNALIZE :: HEART

Reflection Section:

How will this passage change the way I think and feel?

_____

_____

_____

_____

_____

_____

_____

_____

_____

_____

EXTERNALIZE :: HANDS

Application Section:

How will this passage change the way I live?

Key Verse from today:

Silence & Solitude

Spend 30 minutes without speaking and without looking at your phone, TV, or any other technology.
Savor these 30 minutes of stillness.
Aim to direct your thoughts to the Lord and Scripture.
Share your experience below.

Prayer Posture:

5 MINUTE PRAYER WALK

Prayer Focus:

MY FRIENDS

_____

_____

_____

_____

_____

_____

_____

_____

_____

_____

Day 32   Date: _____

Time: _____ Place: _____

Today's Passage
JAMES 1:12-18

OBSERVE :: HEAD

Study Section:

What are the key words, phrases, and
ideas I see in this passage?

_____

_____

_____

_____

_____

_____

_____

_____

_____

_____

_____

INTERNALIZE :: HEART

<u>*Reflection Section:*</u>

How will this passage change the way I
think and feel?

_____

_____

_____

_____

_____

_____

_____

EXTERNALIZE :: HANDS

Application Section:

How will this passage change the way I live?

_____

_____

_____

_____

_____

_____

_____

_____

Key Verse from today:

Silence & Solitude

One benefit of silence is simply searching
the depths of our own souls.
Asking what your blind spots have become
in the rush of everyday life.
Ask yourself:
In the busyness, is there anything important
I'm neglecting or repressing?
What needs refocusing?
Take 10 minutes to ponder these thoughts.
Share your response below.

Prayer Posture:

PRAY WHILE LYING PROSTRATE ON THE FLOOR

Prayer Focus:

MY CURRENT CIRCUMSTANCES & TRIALS

_____

_____

_____

_____

_____

_____

_____

_____

_____

_____

Day 33   Date: _____

Time: _____ Place: _____

Today's Passage
JAMES 1:19-27

<u>OBSERVE :: HEAD</u>

<u>Study Section:</u>

What are the key words, phrases, and
ideas I see in this passage?

_____

_____

_____

_____

_____

_____

_____

_____

_____

INTERNALIZE :: HEART

Reflection Section:

How will this passage change the way I
think and feel?

_____

_____

_____

_____

_____

_____

_____

_____

_____

EXTERNALIZE :: HANDS

Application Section:

How will this passage change the way I live?

_____

_____

_____

_____

_____

_____

_____

Key Verse from today:

Silence & Solitude

Empower your day of silence and solitude by adding a
<u>ONE DAY FAST</u> to your day.
In today's fast, choose to give up something that adds noise to your life.
(i.e. social media, TV, radio, other forms of media, etc.)
Any time you would fill your time with that noise, consciously choose silence to dwell on God and pray.
Share the benefits you experience below.

SIT IN SILENCE & LISTEN TO GOD FOR 5 MINUTES

MY GOALS, DREAMS, & DESIRES

_____

_____

_____

_____

_____

_____

_____

_____

_____

_____

Day 34   Date: _____

Time _____ Place _____

Today's Passage:
REREAD JAMES 1

OBSERVE :: HEAD

Study Section:

Did you see anything new as you read
through the chapter for a 2nd time?

_____

_____

_____

_____

_____

_____

_____

_____

_____

INTERNALIZE :: HEART

Reflection Section:

How will this passage change the way I think and feel?

_____

_____

_____

_____

_____

_____

_____

_____

EXTERNALIZE :: HANDS

Application Section:

How will this passage change the way I live?

_____

_____

_____

_____

_____

_____

_____

Key Verse from today:

Silence & Solitude

Take 10 minutes to listen for God.
After 10 minutes, write down your thoughts
and see what aligns with God's Word.

"Don't assume the voices in your head are
God's; assume they are yours.
To hear God, take up the Scriptures, and
to the degree that your own thoughts for
yourself align with what God has revealed
in His word, then take them as a gift from
God and take them to heart."
(Take a Break from the Chaos,
Desiring God)

Prayer Posture:

FIX YOUR GAZE ON HEAVEN & IMAGINE
STANDING AT THE THRONE OF GRACE

Prayer Focus:

THE SALVATION OF SOMEONE WHO IS
LOST

_____

_____

_____

_____

_____

_____

_____

_____

_____

Day 35   Date: _____

Time: _____ Place: _____

Choose 1 verse to memorize from
JAMES 1

I will memorize...

Prayer Posture:
KNEELING WHILE PRAYING OUT LOUD

_____

_____

_____

_____

What did God teach you during this focused week of silence & solitude?

Welcome to Week 6!

This week's new spiritual discipline is the art of Simplicity.

"The central point for the Discipline of Simplicity is to seek the Kingdom of God and the righteousness of His Kingdom first and then everything necessary will come in its proper order."
– Richard Foster

Deep freedom comes through the Discipline of Simplicity. This discipline begins as an inward determination that results in an outward life-style. This week, we will seek to loosen the grip of material possessions and desires for status and popularity.

May there be no earthly possession that tethers your heart in bondage, rather a spiritual freedom that liberates your heart in devotion to God alone.

Scripture Focus:

JAMES 2

Spiritual Disciplines:

BIBLE STUDY
PRAYER
FASTING
WORSHIP
MEDITATION
SILENCE + SOLITUDE,
& SIMPLICITY

what good is it
my brothers,
if someone says
he has faith
but does not
have works?
CAN THAT FAITH SAVE HIM?

JAMES 2:14

Day 36	Date: _____

Time: _____ Place: _____

Today's Passage
JAMES 2:1-7

OBSERVE :: HEAD

Study Section:

What are the key words, phrases, and
ideas I see in this passage?

_____

_____

_____

_____

_____

_____

_____

_____

_____

_____

INTERNALIZE :: HEART

Reflection Section:

How will this passage change the way I
think and feel?

_____

_____

_____

_____

_____

_____

_____

EXTERNALIZE :: HANDS

Application Section:

How will this passage change the way I live?

Key Verse from today:

Simplify

Read Matthew 6:25-33
"But seek first His kingdom and his righteousness, and all these things shall be yours as well." (vs. 33)

What do you worry most about in life? Oftentimes, our anxiety points to the misplaced priorities in our lives.
Ask God what you are seeking above His Kingdom.
(Example: popularity, money, possessions, appearance, relationships, etc.)
Share below.

Prayer Posture:

PRAY WHILE LYING PROSTRATE ON THE FLOOR

Prayer Focus:

MY COMMUNITY, NATION, AND WORLD

_____

_____

_____

_____

_____

_____

_____

_____

_____

_____

Day 37   Date: _____

Time: _____ Place: _____

Today's Passage

JAMES 2:8-13

OBSERVE :: HEAD

Study Section:

What are the key words, phrases, and ideas I see in this passage?

_____

_____

_____

_____

_____

_____

_____

_____

_____

_____

INTERNALIZE :: HEART

Reflection Section:

How will this passage change the way I think and feel?

_____

_____

_____

_____

_____

_____

_____

_____

_____

EXTERNALIZE :: HANDS

Application Section:

How will this passage change the way I live?

_____

_____

_____

_____

_____

_____

_____

Key Verse from today:

Simplify

For the next week, we will focus on ridding our lives of excess.
First, examine your closet.
Choose 3 possessions from your closet to give to someone in need.
The most powerful way to loosen the grip of excess in your life is by choosing a possession that you truly love, rather than a possession you never think about.
What 3 possessions are you giving away today and to whom?

Prayer Posture:

STAND WITH HANDS LIFTED HIGH

Prayer Focus:

MY FAMILY

_____

_____

_____

_____

_____

_____

_____

_____

_____

_____

_____

_____

Day 38   Date: _____

Time: _____ Place: _____

Today's Passage
JAMES 2:14-17

OBSERVE :: HEAD

Study Section:
_____

What are the key words, phrases, and
ideas I see in this passage?

_____

_____

_____

_____

_____

_____

_____

_____

_____

INTERNALIZE :: HEART

Reflection Section:

How will this passage change the way I
think and feel?

_____

_____

_____

_____

_____

_____

_____

_____

EXTERNALIZE :: HANDS

Application Section:

How will this passage change the way I live?

_____

_____

_____

_____

_____

_____

_____

_____

Key Verse from today:

Simplify

Examine your heart and ask God if
there is anything in your life that is
producing addictive tendencies in you.
(example: soft drinks, Starbucks, junk food,
social media, money, etc)
Simplicity focuses on ridding your heart
of any tether to a possession, activity,
or status level.
How can you reduce this addictive
tendency in your life?
Determine 3 action steps to rid yourself
of this slavery.

Prayer Posture:

KNEEL WITH HANDS OPEN TO HEAVEN

Prayer Focus:

MY FRIENDS

_____

_____

_____

_____

_____

_____

_____

_____

_____

_____

Day 39   Date: _____

Time: _____ Place: _____

Today's Passage
JAMES 2:18-20

OBSERVE :: HEAD

Study Section:
What are the key words, phrases, and
ideas I see in this passage?

_____

_____

_____

_____

_____

_____

_____

_____

_____

_____

_____

INTERNALIZE :: HEART

Reflection Section:

How will this passage change the way I
think and feel?

_____

_____

_____

_____

_____

_____

_____

EXTERNALIZE :: HANDS

Application Section:

How will this passage change the way I live?

_____

_____

_____

_____

_____

_____

_____

Key Verse from today:

Simplify

Develop a habit of giving things away.
"De-accumulate! Masses of things that are not needed complicate life."
- Richard Foster
Look through your household today, and de-accumulate.
Choose 4 possessions to give away.
Share below the 4 possessions you chose and why.

Prayer Posture:

5 MINUTE PRAYER WALK

Prayer Focus:

MY CURRENT CIRCUMSTANCES & TRIALS

_____

_____

_____

_____

_____

_____

_____

_____

_____

_____

Day 40   Date: _____

Time: _____ Place: _____

Today's Passage:
JAMES 2:21-26

OBSERVE :: HEAD

Study Section:

What are the key words, phrases, and
ideas I see in this passage?

_____

_____

_____

_____

_____

_____

_____

_____

_____

INTERNALIZE :: HEART

Reflection Section:

How will this passage change the way I
think and feel?

_____

_____

_____

_____

_____

_____

_____

_____

EXTERNALIZE :: HANDS

Application Section:

How will this passage change the way I
live?

_____

_____

_____

_____

_____

_____

_____

Key Verse from today:

Simplify

Most of the time, technology is an unnecessary drain on energy.
We scroll and scroll, post and post, like and like, and it's all a fairly meaningless use of time.
Delete every social media app from your phone today.
Choose to break the chains of social media for one day. I promise, you'll survive.
Share the benefits you experienced from this act of simplicity below.

Prayer Posture:

FIX YOUR GAZE ON HEAVEN & IMAGINE
STANDING AT THE THRONE OF GRACE

Prayer Focus:

MY GOALS, DREAMS, & DESIRES

_____

_____

_____

_____

_____

_____

_____

_____

_____

_____

Day 41   Date: _____

Time: _____ Place: _____

Today's Passage:
REREAD JAMES 2

OBSERVE :: HEAD

Study Section:
Did you see anything new as you read
through the chapter for a 2nd time?

_____

_____

_____

_____

_____

_____

_____

_____

_____

_____

INTERNALIZE :: HEART

Reflection Section:

How will this passage change the way I
think and feel?

_____

_____

_____

_____

_____

_____

_____

_____

EXTERNALIZE :: HANDS

Application Section:

How will this passage change the way I
live?

_____

_____

_____

_____

_____

_____

_____

_____

Key Verse from today:

Simplify

Part of the art of simplicity is enjoying
the simple things in life.
Today, focus on creation.
Walk outside. Work in the yard. Go on a
hike. Smell the flowers. Visit a garden.
Have a picnic at a park.
Marvel at the beauty of God's creation.
Share your experience below.

Prayer Posture:

SIT IN SILENCE & LISTEN TO GOD FOR 5 MINUTES

Prayer Focus:

THE SALVATION OF SOMEONE WHO IS LOST

_____

_____

_____

_____

_____

_____

_____

_____

_____

Day 42   Date: _____

Time: _____ Place: _____

Choose 1 verse to memorize from
JAMES 2

I will memorize...

Prayer Posture:
KNEELING WHILE PRAYING OUT LOUD

Prayer Focus:

RECENT ANSWERED PRAYERS

_____

_____

_____

_____

How did you benefit from developing the art of simplicity this week?

Welcome to Week 7!

We've reached the halfway point of this journey towards God. I pray that you have experienced the Spirit of God in powerful and personal ways during the past 6 weeks. I pray that your heart has been set on fire by the One and Only Consuming Fire.

Because we are hitting the halfway point, I'd like to revisit the seven spiritual disciplines you've practiced over the last few weeks. Each day we will emphasize one of those disciplines.
I pray that each of these disciplines become a part of your daily life and daily practice.

Let's refresh before I introduce six more new disciplines over the next 6 weeks.

Scripture Focus:

JAMES 3

Spiritual Disciplines:

BIBLE STUDY
PRAYER
FASTING
WORSHIP
MEDITATION
SILENCE + SOLITUDE
& SIMPLICITY

who is wise and
understanding among
you? BY HIS GOOD
CONDUCT LET HIM SHOW
HIS WORKS IN THE
MEEKNESS OF WISDOM.
-James 3:13

Day 43   Date: _____

Time: _____ Place: _____

Today's Passage:
JAMES 3:1-6

OBSERVE :: HEAD

Study Section:

What are the key words, phrases, and
ideas I see in this passage?

_____

_____

_____

_____

_____

_____

_____

_____

_____

_____

INTERNALIZE :: HEART

Reflection Section:

How will this passage change the way I
think and feel?

_____

_____

_____

_____

_____

_____

_____

_____

EXTERNALIZE :: HANDS

Application Section:

How will this passage change the way I live?

_____

_____

_____

_____

_____

_____

_____

_____

Key Verse from today:

Study

As you study today's passage, pick 3 verses that really grab your attention.
Now, find 3 cross references for those 3 verses.
Using cross references in Scripture is my favorite way to go deeper.
It's been said many times, and I believe wholeheartedly:
"Scripture is its own best interpreter."

Example:

James 3:3 → Psalm 32:9

Prayer Posture:

FIX YOUR GAZE ON HEAVEN & IMAGINE
STANDING AT THE THRONE OF GRACE

Prayer Focus:

MY COMMUNITY,
NATION, AND WORLD

_____

_____

_____

_____

_____

_____

_____

_____

_____

Day 44	Date: _____

Time: _____ Place: _____

Today's Passage
JAMES 3:7-12

OBSERVE :: HEAD

Study Section:

What are the key words, phrases, and ideas I see in this passage?

_____

_____

_____

_____

_____

_____

_____

_____

_____

INTERNALIZE :: HEART

Reflection Section:

How will this passage change the way I think and feel?

_____

_____

_____

_____

_____

_____

_____

_____

EXTERNALIZE :: HANDS

Application Section:

How will this passage change the way I live?

_____

_____

_____

_____

_____

_____

_____

_____

Key Verse from today:

Pray

Spend 15 uninterrupted minutes in prayer.

During the 15 minutes, spend at least 5 minutes listening for God.

"A man prayed, and at first he thought that prayer was talking. But he became more and more quiet until in the end he realized that prayer is listening."

- Soren Kierkegaard

What did you pray about? What did you hear from God?

Prayer Posture:

PRAY WHILE LYING PROSTRATE ON THE
FLOOR

Prayer Focus:

MY FAMILY

_____

_____

_____

_____

_____

_____

_____

_____

_____

_____

Day 45   Date: _____

Time: _____ Place: _____

Today's Passage:
JAMES 3:1-12

OBSERVE :: HEAD

Study Section:

What are the key words, phrases, and ideas I see in this passage?

_____

_____

_____

_____

_____

_____

_____

_____

_____

_____

INTERNALIZE :: HEART

Reflection Section:

How will this passage change the way I
think and feel?

_____

_____

_____

_____

_____

_____

_____

_____

_____

EXTERNALIZE :: HANDS

Application Section:

How will this passage change the way I live?

Key Verse from today:

Worship

"To worship is to experience Reality, to touch Life. It is to know, to feel, to experience the resurrected Christ in the midst of the gathered community. It is a breaking into the Shekinah of God, or better yet, being invaded by the Shekinah of God."
- Richard Foster

"Shekinah" means the glory or radiance of God dwelling in the midst of his people. It denotes the immediate Presence of God as opposed to a God who is abstract or aloof.

Spend 15 minutes in worship, singing in exaltation to God.

As you worship, imagine a picture of His glory and radiance. Focus, with that picture at the forefront of your mind during the next 15 minutes.

Reflect on this time of worship:

Prayer Posture:

STAND WITH HANDS LIFTED HIGH

Prayer Focus:

MY FRIENDS

_____

_____

_____

_____

_____

_____

_____

_____

_____

_____

Day 46   Date: _____

Time: _____ Place: _____

Today's Passage:
JAMES 3:13-16

OBSERVE :: HEAD

Study Section:

What are the key words, phrases, and
ideas I see in this passage?

_____

_____

_____

_____

_____

_____

_____

_____

_____

_____

INTERNALIZE :: HEART

Reflection Section:

How will this passage change the way I
think and feel?

_____

_____

_____

_____

_____

_____

_____

EXTERNALIZE :: HANDS

Application Section:

How will this passage change the way I live?

_____

_____

_____

_____

_____

_____

_____

Key Verse from today:

Meditate

The Word of God is like a love letter addressed to you. As you meditate upon Scripture, view God's Words in that way.
"Just as you do not analyze the words of someone you love, but accept them as they are said to you, accept the Word of Scripture and ponder it in your heart, as Mary did. That is all. That is meditation."
– Dietrich Bonhoeffer

Spend 5 minutes meditating on today's verses. Enter into the passage. Instead of dissecting the words, let the words take root in your heart.
What did you learn?

Prayer Posture:
5 MINUTE PRAYER WALK

Prayer Focus:
MY CURRENT CIRCUMSTANCES & TRIALS

_____

_____

_____

_____

_____

_____

_____

_____

_____

_____

Day 47   Date: _____

Time: _____ Place: _____

Today's Passage:
JAMES 3:17-18

OBSERVE :: HEAD

Study Section:

What are the key words, phrases, and ideas I see in this passage?

_____

_____

_____

_____

_____

_____

_____

_____

_____

INTERNALIZE :: HEART

Reflection Section:

How will this passage change the way I think and feel?

_____

_____

_____

_____

_____

_____

_____

_____

EXTERNALIZE :: HANDS

Application Section:

How will this passage change the way I live?

_____

_____

_____

_____

_____

_____

_____

Key Verse from today:

Silence & Solitude

Go on a 10 minute retreat.
(Go for a walk by yourself, go for a silent drive, sit under a tree, lock yourself in a closet. Anything you need to do to get alone for 10 minutes.)

"There is a freedom to be alone, not in order to be away from people but in order to hear the divine Whisper better."
- Richard Foster

Sink into the silence and solitude of God.

No specific agenda. No to-do's. Just a time to rest in the silence and solitude of God's Presence.

How was this experience? Share below.

Prayer Posture:

KNEEL WITH HANDS OPEN TO HEAVEN

Prayer Focus:

MY GOALS, DREAMS, & DESIRES

_____

_____

_____

_____

_____

_____

_____

_____

_____

_____

Day 48   Date: _____

Time _____ Place _____

Today's Passage:
REREAD JAMES 3

OBSERVE :: HEAD

Study Section:

Did you see anything new as you read
through the chapter for a 2nd time?

_____

_____

_____

_____

_____

_____

_____

_____

_____

INTERNALIZE :: HEART

Reflection Section:

How will this passage change the way I think and feel?

_____

_____

_____

_____

_____

_____

_____

_____

EXTERNALIZE :: HANDS

Application Section:

How will this passage change the way I live?

_____

_____

_____

_____

_____

_____

_____

_____

Key Verse from today:

Simplify

Omit all extra-technology from your day today.
Delete at least one social media app from your phone today, turn off the TV, don't watch a single show on Netflix.
Fill that time with something simple.
(Example: a conversation with a friend, a walk by yourself, playing with your child, etc.)

Did you feel a sense of freedom?
Explain below.

Prayer Posture:
SIT IN SILENCE & LISTEN TO GOD FOR 5 MINUTES

Prayer Focus:
THE SALVATION OF SOMEONE WHO IS LOST

_____

_____

_____

_____

_____

_____

_____

_____

_____

_____

Day 49   Date: _____

Time: _____ Place: _____

Choose 1 verse to memorize from
JAMES 3

I will memorize...

Prayer Posture:
KNEELING WHILE PRAYING OUT LOUD

_____

_____

_____

_____

Which spiritual discipline comes most naturally to you? Which discipline is the most difficult for you?

Welcome to Week 8!

In week 8, we will practice the Discipline of Surrender.

The Discipline of Surrender means we trust our Lord Jesus Christ in all things without doubt or fault in our faith. We let go of our hold on our perceived rights, agendas, and opinions that are not lined up to His. In this way, we can surrender to His love and embrace God's will for our lives, live His Way in holiness, and become a benefit to the lives of others. We come before God and under new management – His. The Discipline of Surrender is a discipline because we have to make it a daily decision and practice.
(*The Discipline of Surrender by Dr. Richard J. Krejcir http://www.discipleshiptools.org*)

Surrender, by definition, means relinquishing control.

Therefore, this week, we will be
practicing the act of giving up control.

Scripture Focus:

JAMES 4

Spiritual Disciplines:

BIBLE STUDY
PRAYER
FASTING
WORSHIP
MEDITATION
SILENCE + SOLITUDE
SIMPLICITY
& SURRENDER

submit
yourselves
to God.
RESIST THE DEVIL,
and he
will flee
from you.

– JAMES 4:7

Day 50   Date: _____

Time _____   Place _____

Today's Passage:
JAMES 4:1-3

OBSERVE :: HEAD

Study Section:

What are the key words, phrases, and
ideas I see in this passage?

_____

_____

_____

_____

_____

_____

_____

_____

_____

INTERNALIZE :: HEART

_____

_____

_____

_____

_____

_____

_____

EXTERNALIZE :: HANDS

Application Section:

How will this passage change the way I
live?

_____

_____

_____

_____

_____

_____

_____

_____

Key Verse from today:

Surrender

> "The reason why many are still troubled, still seeking, still making little forward progress is because they haven't yet come to the end of themselves. We're still trying to give orders, and interfering with God's work within us."
> – A.W. Tozer

First, surrender means recognizing the lie that we are in control, and admitting the truth that we are not.
How do you try to live like you are in control?
Share below.

Prayer Posture:

KNEEL WITH HANDS OPEN TO HEAVEN

Prayer Focus:

MY COMMUNITY,
NATION, AND WORLD

_____

_____

_____

_____

_____

_____

_____

_____

_____

_____

Day 51   Date: _____

Time: _____ Place: _____

Today's Passage
JAMES 4:4-6

<u>OBSERVE :: HEAD</u>

Study Section:

What are the key words, phrases, and
ideas I see in this passage?

_____

_____

_____

_____

_____

_____

_____

_____

_____

_____

INTERNALIZE :: HEART

Reflection Section:

How will this passage change the way I think and feel?

_____

_____

_____

_____

_____

_____

_____

_____

_____

EXTERNALIZE :: HANDS

Application Section:

How will this passage change the way I live?

_____

_____

_____

_____

_____

_____

_____

Key Verse from today:

Surrender

> "Fallen man is not simply an imperfect creature who needs improvement: he is a rebel who must lay down his arms. Laying down your arms, surrendering, saying you are sorry, realizing that you have been on the wrong track and getting ready to start life over again from the ground floor-that is the only way out of a 'hole.' This process of surrender-this movement full speed astern-is repentance."
> – C.S. Lewis

Second, surrender means dying to your old way of life – dying to a life of sin. Take 5 minutes, examining your heart through the eyes of the Holy Spirit, and ask God to reveal sins you need to repent of and surrender.
Share below what He reveals.

Prayer Posture:

STAND WITH HANDS LIFTED HIGH

Prayer Focus:

MY FAMILY

_____

_____

_____

_____

_____

_____

_____

_____

_____

_____

Day 52   Date: _____

Time: _____ Place: _____

Today's Passage:
JAMES 4:7-10

OBSERVE :: HEAD

Study Section:

What are the key words, phrases, and
ideas I see in this passage?

_____

_____

_____

_____

_____

_____

_____

_____

_____

INTERNALIZE :: HEART

Reflection Section:

How will this passage change the way I think and feel?

_____

_____

_____

_____

_____

_____

_____

_____

_____

EXTERNALIZE :: HANDS

Application Section:

How will this passage change the way I live?

_____

_____

_____

_____

_____

_____

_____

Key Verse from today:

Surrender

"You cannot fulfill God's purposes for your life while focusing on your own plans."
– Rick Warren

The next step in surrender is surrendering your will to the will of our loving God. Write down your habits, your plans, your desires, and your hopes. Pray a prayer of surrender, and ask God to reveal where your will does not align with His will for your life.

My will (my habits, plans, desires, hopes):

My prayer of surrender:

"Yet not my will, but Yours be done."
(Luke 22:42)

Where does my will conflict with your will?

Prayer Posture:

PRAY WHILE LYING PROSTRATE ON THE FLOOR

Prayer Focus:

MY FRIENDS

Day 53

Date: _____

Time: _____   Place: _____

Today's Passage:
JAMES 4:11-12

OBSERVE :: HEAD

Study Section:

What are the key words, phrases, and ideas I see in this passage?

_____

_____

_____

_____

_____

_____

_____

_____

_____

_____

INTERNALIZE :: HEART

Reflection Section:

How will this passage change the way I
think and feel?

_____

_____

_____

_____

_____

_____

_____

EXTERNALIZE :: HANDS

Application Section:

How will this passage change the way I live?

_____

_____

_____

_____

_____

_____

_____

Key Verse from today:

Surrender

Next, we're going to work through a list
of areas in which we must surrender to
become fully free.
Jot down the things that are most
difficult to surrender in each area and
why.

My possession:

My health:

My family:

Prayer Posture:

5 MINUTE PRAYER WALK

Prayer Focus:

MY CURRENT CIRCUMSTANCES & TRIALS

_____

_____

_____

_____

_____

_____

_____

_____

_____

Day 54   Date: _____

Time: _____ Place: _____

Today's Passage:
JAMES 4:13-17

OBSERVE :: HEAD

Study Section:

What are the key words, phrases, and
ideas I see in this passage?

_____

_____

_____

_____

_____

_____

_____

_____

_____

_____

INTERNALIZE :: HEART

Reflection Section:

How will this passage change the way I
think and feel?

_____

_____

_____

_____

_____

_____

_____

_____

EXTERNALIZE :: HANDS

Application Section:

How will this passage change the way I live?

_____

_____

_____

_____

_____

_____

_____

Key Verse from today:

Surrender

"The more we let God take us over, the more truly ourselves we become — because he made us. He invented all the different people that you and I were intended to be. It is when I turn to Christ, when I give up myself to His personality, that I first begin to have a real personality of my own."
– C.S. Lewis

Next, ask God to reveal any anxiety, fear, stress, pride, or tension that well up in your heart when trying to surrender. Share below what God reveals.

Prayer Posture:
FIX YOUR GAZE ON HEAVEN & IMAGINE
STANDING AT THE THRONE OF GRACE

Prayer Focus:
MY GOALS, DREAMS, & DESIRES

_____

_____

_____

_____

_____

_____

_____

_____

_____

_____

Day 55   Date: _____

Time: _____ Place: _____

Today's Passage:
REREAD JAMES 4

OBSERVE :: HEAD

Study Section:

Did you see anything new as you read
through the chapter for a 2nd time?

_____

_____

_____

_____

_____

_____

_____

_____

_____

_____

INTERNALIZE :: HEART

_____

_____

_____

_____

_____

_____

_____

_____

_____

EXTERNALIZE :: HANDS

Application Section:

How will this passage change the way I
live?

_____

_____

_____

_____

_____

_____

_____

_____

Key Verse from today:

Surrender

> "If you cling to your life, you will lose it; but if you give up your life for me, you will find it."
> Matthew 10:39

Share with a trusted family member, friend, or accountability partner what areas of your life you're seeking to surrender more fully. Ask this trusted confidant to help keep you accountable in this area of surrender.

I am clinging to:

I am giving up control by the power of Your Spirit.

Prayer Posture:

SIT IN SILENCE & LISTEN TO GOD FOR 5 MINUTES

Prayer Focus:

THE SALVATION OF SOMEONE WHO IS LOST

_____

_____

_____

_____

_____

_____

_____

_____

Day 56   Date: _____

Time: _____ Place: _____

Choose 1 verse to memorize from
JAMES 4

I will memorize...

Prayer Posture:
KNEELING WHILE PRAYING OUT LOUD

_____

_____

_____

_____

Lord, I commit to daily surrendering the following areas of my life by the power of your Spirit:

In week 9, we will put into practice the Discipline of Service.

First, I must distinguish between self-righteous service and true service. Self-righteous service stems from human effort, while true service stems from a relationship with God through the power of His Spirit. True service is born out of whispered promptings and divine urgings from the Spirit. Self-righteous service picks and chooses whom to serve, while true service can serve enemies as freely as it serves friends.

Second, understand that of all the disciplines, service is the most conducive to the growth of humility in your life. "Nothing disciplines the inordinate desires of the flesh like service, and nothing transforms the desires of the flesh like serving in hiddenness."

- Richard Foster, *The Celebration of Discipline*

This week, as we find practical ways of serving, begin each action by testing your heart and your motives. Ask God to prompt you and lead you as you seek to serve others in humility, without expecting anything in return.

Scripture Focus:

JAMES 5

Spiritual Disciplines:

BIBLE STUDY
PRAYER
FASTING
WORSHIP
MEDITATION
SILENCE + SOLITUDE
SIMPLICITY
SURRENDER
& SERVICE

Therefore, confess
your sins to one
another and pray
for one another, that
you may be healed.
The prayer of a
righteous person
has great power
as it is working.
—James 5:16

Day 57　　　　　Date: _____

Time: _____ Place: _____

Today's Passage
JAMES 5:1-6

OBSERVE :: HEAD

Study Section:

What are the key words, phrases, and
ideas I see in this passage?

_____

_____

_____

_____

_____

_____

_____

_____

_____

INTERNALIZE :: HEART

Reflection Section:

How will this passage change the way I
think and feel?

_____

_____

_____

_____

_____

_____

_____

_____

EXTERNALIZE :: HANDS

Application Section:

How will this passage change the way I live?

_____

_____

_____

_____

_____

_____

_____

Key Verse from today:

Serve

In our first act of service this week, find someone to serve through <u>hiddenness.</u>
Open your eyes, and ask God to reveal someone who needs to be shown a hidden act of service.

Maybe it's an unseen peer at school, maybe it's a discouraged friend, maybe a stranger, maybe an exhausted parent.

Find a way to serve that person in a hidden way.

Share your experience below.

Prayer Posture:

STAND WITH HANDS LIFTED HIGH

Prayer Focus:

MY COMMUNITY,
NATION, AND WORLD

_____

_____

_____

_____

_____

_____

_____

_____

_____

Day 58   Date: _____

Time: _____ Place: _____

Today's Passage:
JAMES 5:7-12

OBSERVE :: HEAD

Study Section:

What are the key words, phrases, and
ideas I see in this passage?

_____

_____

_____

_____

_____

_____

_____

_____

_____

_____

INTERNALIZE :: HEART

Reflection Section:

How will this passage change the way I think and feel?

_____

_____

_____

_____

_____

_____

_____

_____

_____

EXTERNALIZE :: HANDS

Application Section:

How will this passage change the way I live?

_____

_____

_____

_____

_____

_____

_____

Key Verse from today:

Serve

> "The second service that one should perform for another in a Christian community is that of active helpfulness. This means, initially, simply assistance in trifling, external matters. There is a multitude of these things wherever people live together."
> – Dietrich Bonhoeffer

Second, find a way to serve someone in your home in a <u>small, helpful way.</u> Perhaps ask a family member, how you could help them. Maybe do the dishes or laundry without being asked. Think of the most surprising, yet practical way you can help someone in your family unit today, and do it.
Share your experience below.

Prayer Posture:

KNEEL WITH HANDS OPEN TO HEAVEN

Prayer Focus:

MY FAMILY

_____

_____

_____

_____

_____

_____

_____

_____

_____

_____

_____

Day 59   Date: _____

Time: _____   Place: _____

Today's Passage:
JAMES 5:13-15

OBSERVE :: HEAD

Study Section:

What are the key words, phrases, and
ideas I see in this passage?

_____

_____

_____

_____

_____

_____

_____

_____

_____

_____

INTERNALIZE :: HEART

Reflection Section:

How will this passage change the way I
think and feel?

_____

_____

_____

_____

_____

_____

_____

_____

EXTERNALIZE :: HANDS

Application Section:

How will this passage change the way I live?

_____

_____

_____

_____

_____

_____

_____

Key Verse from today:

Serve

"Guarding the reputation of others is a deep
and lasting service."
- Richard Foster

Today's act of service is to <u>guard the
reputation of others</u>. We have all been
a part of gossip, and most of us have
been the victim of gossip. There is great
discipline in holding one's tongue, and
there is even greater discipline in
defending those who are being
slandered. This may be one of the
greatest acts of service you can
participate in for another.

How can you participate in this
discipline today? Share below.

"Don't tell me what they said about me. Tell me
why they were so comfortable to say it
around you." - Shelley Giglio

Prayer Posture:

5 MINUTE PRAYER WALK

Prayer Focus:

MY FRIENDS

_____

_____

_____

_____

_____

_____

_____

_____

_____

_____

_____

Day 60   Date: _____

Time: _____ Place: _____

Today's Passage
JAMES 5:16-18

OBSERVE :: HEAD

Study Section:

What are the key words, phrases, and
ideas I see in this passage?

_____

_____

_____

_____

_____

_____

_____

_____

_____

_____

_____

INTERNALIZE :: HEART

Reflection Section:

How will this passage change the way I
think and feel?

_____

_____

_____

_____

_____

_____

_____

EXTERNALIZE :: HANDS

Application Section:

How will this passage change the way I live?

_____

_____

_____

_____

_____

_____

_____

Key Verse from today:

Serve

"Practice hospitality ungrudgingly to one another." - 1 Peter 4:9

Today, we will practice the service of
<u>hospitality</u>.
Who can you invite into your home?
Who do you see that could use a sense
of family and love? Don't
overcomplicate hospitality.
Just embrace, invite, and share
meaningful time with others.
Share your experience below.

Prayer Posture:
PRAY WHILE LYING PROSTRATE ON THE FLOOR

Prayer Focus:
MY CURRENT CIRCUMSTANCES & TRIALS

_____

_____

_____

_____

_____

_____

_____

_____

_____

_____

Day 61   Date: _____

Time: _____   Place: _____

Today's Passage:
JAMES 5:19-20

OBSERVE :: HEAD

Study Section:

What are the key words, phrases, and
ideas I see in this passage?

_____

_____

_____

_____

_____

_____

_____

_____

_____

_____

INTERNALIZE :: HEART

Reflection Section:

How will this passage change the way I
think and feel?

_____

_____

_____

_____

_____

_____

_____

_____

EXTERNALIZE :: HANDS

Application Section:

How will this passage change the way I live?

_____

_____

_____

_____

_____

_____

_____

Key Verse from today:

Serve

> "There is a kind of listening with half an ear that presumes already to know what the other person has to say. It is an impatient, inattentive listening, that despises the brother and is only waiting for a chance to speak and thus get rid of the other person. This is no fulfillment of our obligation, and it is certain that here too our attitude toward our brother only reflects our relationship to God. Christians have forgotten that the ministry of listening has been committed to them by Him who is Himself the great listener and whose work they should share. We should listen with the ears of God that we may speak the Word of God."
> – Dietrich Bonhoeffer

Next, we will participate in the service of listening. Who can you seek out to patiently and selflessly listen to today? Share your experience below.

Prayer Posture:

SIT IN SILENCE & LISTEN TO GOD FOR 5 MINUTES

Prayer Focus:

MY GOALS, DREAMS, & DESIRES

_____

_____

_____

_____

_____

_____

_____

_____

_____

_____

Day 62   Date: _____

Time: _____   Place: _____

Today's Passage:
REREAD JAMES 5

OBSERVE :: HEAD

Study Section:
Did you see anything new as you read
through the chapter for a 2nd time?

_____

_____

_____

_____

_____

_____

_____

_____

_____

INTERNALIZE :: HEART

Reflection Section:

How will this passage change the way I
think and feel?

_____

_____

_____

_____

_____

_____

_____

_____

_____

EXTERNALIZE :: HANDS

Application Section:

How will this passage change the way I live?

_____

_____

_____

_____

_____

_____

_____

_____

Key Verse from today:

Serve

"Bear one another's burdens, and so fulfill the
law of Christ."
Galatians 6:2

Today, we serve by bearing the
burdens of each other. Do you know
someone who is walking through a
difficult time? Find a way to show your
love and concern. Find a way to carry
a portion of the weight of their burden.
Maybe you can serve this person by
writing a note, making a call, or visiting
their house.
Share your experience below.

Prayer Posture:

FIX YOUR GAZE ON HEAVEN & IMAGINE
STANDING AT THE THRONE OF GRACE

Prayer Focus:

THE SALVATION OF SOMEONE WHO IS
LOST

Day 63   Date: _____

Time: _____ Place: _____

Choose 1 verse to memorize from
JAMES 5

I will memorize...

Prayer Posture:
KNEELING WHILE PRAYING OUT LOUD

Prayer Focus:

RECENT ANSWERED PRAYERS

_____

_____

_____

_____

Commit to this prayer everyday:

"Lord Jesus, as it would please you bring me someone today whom I can serve."

I commit to walk in this way.

Sign: _____

Date: _____

Welcome to Week 10!

This week's new spiritual discipline is the Discipline of Confession. I'm sure as many of you read that, you begin to feel uncomfortable. Confession is not an easy discipline, but it is absolutely imperative to our spiritual growth. Nothing causes more of a drought in your spiritual life than unconfessed sin. Unconfessed sin has a way of lingering and festering in our souls, causing us to harden our hearts and close ourselves off from God. Unconfessed sin acts as a brick-wall barrier between our hearts and the heart of God.

Therefore, we must daily ask God to search us and expose any way in us that is not of Him.

"Even if I caused you sorrow by my letter, I do not regret it. Though I did regret it—I see that my letter hurt you, but only for a little while—

yet now I am happy, not because you were made sorry, but because your sorrow led you to repentance. For you became sorrowful as God intended and so were not harmed in any way by us. Godly sorrow brings repentance that leads to salvation and leaves no regret, but worldly sorrow brings death."
2 Corinthians 7:8-10

"For a good confession three things are necessary: an examination of conscience, sorrow, and a determination to avoid sin."
St. Alphonsus Liguori

As we enter into this week, we will be engaging in these different steps toward confession:

1. Examination of the Conscience
2. Sorrow for Sin
3. A Determination to Avoid Sin
4. An Acceptance of Forgiveness & Freedom from Sin

Scripture Focus:

I JOHN 1 & 2

Spiritual Disciplines:

BIBLE STUDY
PRAYER
FASTING
WORSHIP
MEDITATION
SILENCE + SOLITUDE
SIMPLICITY
SURRENDER
SERVICE
& CONFESSION

if we CONFESS our
sins, He is FAITHFUL
and JUST TO FORGIVE
us our sins and
to CLEANSE us from
all UNRIGTEOUSNESS.
— 1 john 1:9 —

Day 64   Date: _____

Time: _____   Place: _____

Today's Passage:
1 JOHN 1:1-4

OBSERVE :: HEAD

Study Section:

What are the key words, phrases, and
ideas I see in this passage?

_____

_____

_____

_____

_____

_____

_____

_____

_____

_____

INTERNALIZE :: HEART

Reflection Section:

How will this passage change the way I think and feel?

_____

_____

_____

_____

_____

_____

_____

_____

EXTERNALIZE :: HANDS

Application Section:

How will this passage change the way I live?

_____

_____

_____

_____

_____

_____

_____

Key Verse from today:

Confess

Read Hebrews 4:12-13
"For the word of God is full of living power. It is sharper than the sharpest knife, cutting deep into our innermost thoughts and desires. It exposes us for what we really are. Nothing in all creation can hide from him. Everything is naked and exposed before his eyes. This is the God to whom we must explain all that we have done."

For 5 minutes, lay yourself bare before God. Allow the Holy Spirit to expose your true heart.
Is God convicting you of anything?
Please share below.

Prayer Posture:
KNEEL WITH HANDS OPEN TO HEAVEN

Prayer Focus:
MY COMMUNITY,
NATION, AND WORLD

_____

_____

_____

_____

_____

_____

_____

_____

_____

Day 65   Date: _____

Time _____ Place _____

Today's Passage
I JOHN 1:5-10

<u>OBSERVE :: HEAD</u>

Study Section:

What are the key words, phrases, and
ideas I see in this passage?

_____

_____

_____

_____

_____

_____

_____

_____

_____

_____

INTERNALIZE :: HEART

Reflection Section:

How will this passage change the way I
think and feel?

_____

_____

_____

_____

_____

_____

_____

_____

EXTERNALIZE :: HANDS

Application Section:

How will this passage change the way I
live?

_____

_____

_____

_____

_____

_____

_____

Key Verse from today:

Confess

Confession simply means <u>to agree with God</u>. He already sees and knows our sins. The barrier between you and God comes when you're unwilling to admit, acknowledge, and agree with Him about your sin.

Read Luke 12:2

"Everything that is hidden will be shown, and everything that is secret will be made known."

What are you trying to hide? What won't you admit? How can you agree with God about your sin today?

Prayer Posture:

5 MINUTE PRAYER WALK

Prayer Focus:

MY FAMILY

_____

_____

_____

_____

_____

_____

_____

_____

_____

_____

do not love this world nor the things it offers you, for when you love the world, you do not have the love of the Father in you.

first john two: fifteen

Day 66   Date: _____

Time: _____ Place: _____

Today's Passage
1 JOHN 2:1-6

OBSERVE :: HEAD

Study Section:

What are the key words, phrases, and
ideas I see in this passage?

_____

_____

_____

_____

_____

_____

_____

_____

_____

INTERNALIZE :: HEART

_____

_____

_____

_____

_____

_____

_____

_____

_____

EXTERNALIZE :: HANDS

Application Section:

How will this passage change the way I live?

_____

_____

_____

_____

_____

_____

_____

Key Verse from today:

Confess

Read Psalm 32:3-5

"When I refused to confess my sin, I was weak and miserable, and I groaned all day long. Day and night your hand of discipline was heavy on me. My strength evaporated like water in the summer heart. Finally, I confessed all my sins to you and stopped trying to hide them. I said to myself, 'I will confess my rebellion to the Lord.' And you forgave me! All my guilt is gone."

What effects do you feel from unconfessed sin?

What freedom do you feel from confessing your sin?

Prayer Posture:

PRAY WHILE LYING PROSTRATE ON THE
FLOOR

Prayer Focus:

MY FRIENDS

_____

_____

_____

_____

_____

_____

_____

_____

_____

_____

Day 67   Date: _____

Time: _____ Place: _____

Today's Passage:
1 JOHN 2:7-14

OBSERVE :: HEAD

Study Section:

What are the key words, phrases, and
ideas I see in this passage?

_____

_____

_____

_____

_____

_____

_____

_____

_____

_____

INTERNALIZE :: HEART

Reflection Section:

How will this passage change the way I
think and feel?

_____

_____

_____

_____

_____

_____

_____

EXTERNALIZE :: HANDS

Application Section:

How will this passage change the way I live?

_____

_____

_____

_____

_____

_____

_____

Key Verse from today:

Confess

1. Write down the main area of sin you are struggling with lately.
2. Take 3 minutes to meditate on the seriousness and the effects of this sin.
3. Choose one trusted person to admit this struggle to as an action of repentance and a desire for accountability.
4. Write down 4 practical ways you are determined to avoid and turn from this sin.

Prayer Posture:

STAND WITH HANDS LIFTED HIGH

Prayer Focus:

MY CURRENT CIRCUMSTANCES & TRIALS

_____

_____

_____

_____

_____

_____

_____

_____

_____

_____

_____

_____

Day 68   Date: _____

Time: _____   Place: _____

Today's Passage
1 JOHN 2:15-17

OBSERVE :: HEAD

Study Section:

What are the key words, phrases, and
ideas I see in this passage?

_____

_____

_____

_____

_____

_____

_____

_____

_____

INTERNALIZE :: HEART

Reflection Section:

How will this passage change the way I
think and feel?

_____

_____

_____

_____

_____

_____

_____

_____

EXTERNALIZE :: HANDS

Application Section:

How will this passage change the way I
live?

_____

_____

_____

_____

_____

_____

_____

Key Verse from today:

Confess

Read Acts 3:19
"Repent, then, and turn to God, so that your sins may be wiped out, that times of refreshing may come from the Lord."
After repenting of your sin and turning to God, describe the kind of freedom and refreshment that have come from a clear conscience.
Take 5 minutes to reflect on the freedom you have found through confession.

Prayer Posture:

KNEELING WHILE PRAYING OUT LOUD

Prayer Focus:

MY GOALS, DREAMS, & DESIRES

_____

_____

_____

_____

_____

_____

_____

_____

_____

_____

Day 69   Date: _____

Time: _____ Place: _____

Today's Passage:
1 JOHN 2:18-29

OBSERVE :: HEAD

Study Section:

Did you see anything new as you read
through the chapter for a 2nd time?

_____

_____

_____

_____

_____

_____

_____

_____

_____

INTERNALIZE :: HEART

Reflection Section:

How will this passage change the way I think and feel?

_____

_____

_____

_____

_____

_____

_____

_____

EXTERNALIZE :: HANDS

Application Section:

How will this passage change the way I live?

Key Verse from today:

Confess

Take 5 minutes to reflect and rejoice in the Lord for His willingness to pour out undeserved mercy, grace, forgiveness, and love for you!
Write down your praises.
(Read Psalm 32 for inspiration.)

Prayer Posture:

SIT IN SILENCE & LISTEN TO GOD FOR 5 MINUTES

Prayer Focus:

THE SALVATION OF SOMEONE WHO IS LOST

_____

_____

_____

_____

_____

_____

_____

_____

_____

Day 70   Date: _____

Time: _____   Place: _____

Today's Passage:
REREAD JOHN 1 & 2

OBSERVE :: HEAD

Study Section:
Did you see anything new as you read
through the chapter for a 2nd time?

_____

_____

_____

_____

_____

_____

_____

_____

_____

_____

INTERNALIZE :: HEART

Reflection Section:

How will this passage change the way I
think and feel?

_____

_____

_____

_____

_____

_____

EXTERNALIZE :: HANDS

Application Section:

How will this passage change the way I
live?

_____

_____

_____

_____

_____

_____

_____

Key Verse from today:

Prayer Posture:

FIX YOUR GAZE ON HEAVEN & IMAGINE
STANDING AT THE THRONE OF GRACE

Prayer Focus:

RECENT ANSWERED PRAYERS

_____

_____

_____

_____

What did God reveal to you about your heart during this week?

Welcome to Week 11!

This week, we will focus on the Discipline of Guidance.

The Discipline of Guidance manifests itself both through the individual pursuit of guidance from God and the corporate pursuit of guidance from God.

The Disciplines of Solitude, Silence, Prayer, and Meditation all prepare us for listening to God. The Discipline of Guidance helps us to develop the spiritual ears and eyes that are necessary for hearing and seeing God's direction for our lives.

An important aspect of the Discipline of Guidance is learning to listen to the guidance of the Holy Spirit through what others in the body of Christ are saying and doing.
- Michael Bischof, Souleader Resources

"God's purpose in guidance is not to get us to perform the right actions. His purpose is to help us become the right kind of people." –
John Ortberg

Scripture Focus:

1 JOHN 3

Spiritual Disciplines:

BIBLE STUDY
PRAYER
FASTING
WORSHIP
MEDITATION
SILENCE + SOLITUDE
SIMPLICITY
SURRENDER
SERVICE
CONFESSION
& GUIDANCE

See how great a love
the Father has bestowed
on us, that we would
be called children
of God; and such we
are. For this reason
the world does not
know us, because it
did not know Him.

-1 JOHN 3:1

Day 71   Date: _____

Time: _____   Place: _____

Today's Passage
1 JOHN 3:1-6

OBSERVE :: HEAD

Study Section:
_____

What are the key words, phrases, and
ideas I see in this passage?

_____

_____

_____

_____

_____

_____

_____

_____

_____

_____

INTERNALIZE :: HEART

Reflection Section:

How will this passage change the way I
think and feel?

_____

_____

_____

_____

_____

_____

_____

_____

EXTERNALIZE :: HANDS

Application Section:

How will this passage change the way I live?

_____

_____

_____

_____

_____

_____

_____

Key Verse from today:

Guidance

Take 5 minutes to think and pray about the top 5 things you believe God is calling you to do (or stop doing) in life. (This could be in the immediate or distant future.)
Write down those top 5 things:

God is calling me to...

1.

2.

3.

4.

5.

Prayer Posture:

KNEEL WITH HANDS OPEN TO HEAVEN

Prayer Focus:

MY COMMUNITY,
NATION, AND WORLD

_____

_____

_____

_____

_____

_____

_____

_____

Day 72   Date: _____

Time: _____ Place: _____

Today's Passage:
1 JOHN 3:7-10

OBSERVE :: HEAD

Study Section:

What are the key words, phrases, and ideas I see in this passage?

_____

_____

_____

_____

_____

_____

_____

_____

_____

INTERNALIZE :: HEART

Reflection Section:
_____

How will this passage change the way I
think and feel?

_____

_____

_____

_____

_____

_____

_____

_____

EXTERNALIZE :: HANDS

Application Section:

How will this passage change the way I live?

_____

_____

_____

_____

_____

_____

_____

Key Verse from today:

Guidance

Throughout this week, we will refer back to the top 5 things you wrote down yesterday.

Today, ask God if any of those things you wrote down were of your own creation or if they are truly God's call on your life.

Take 5 minutes to listen for God.

Share your thoughts below.

Prayer Posture:
PRAY WHILE LYING PROSTRATE ON THE FLOOR

Prayer Focus:
MY FAMILY

_____

_____

_____

_____

_____

_____

_____

_____

_____

_____

Day 73   Date: _____

Time: _____   Place: _____

Today's Passage:
1 JOHN 3:11-13

OBSERVE :: HEAD

Study Section:

What are the key words, phrases, and
ideas I see in this passage?

_____

_____

_____

_____

_____

_____

_____

_____

_____

INTERNALIZE :: HEART

Reflection Section:

How will this passage change the way I
think and feel?

_____

_____

_____

_____

_____

_____

_____

_____

_____

EXTERNALIZE :: HANDS

Application Section:

How will this passage change the way I live?

_____

_____

_____

_____

_____

_____

_____

Key Verse from today:

Guidance

An excellent way to practice the Discipline of Guidance is through the influence of a spiritual director (a mentor or discipleship leader).

If you do not already have someone who functions as a spiritual director in your life, consider finding one as soon as possible.

Take 10 minutes to begin praying about who your spiritual director should be.

Think of someone you know and admire.
Someone who is older and wiser than you.
Someone of the same gender.
Someone you trust wholeheartedly.

Once the Lord has clearly placed someone on your heart, contact that person and ask if they would be willing to be your spiritual mentor.

(Do not rush this process, pray through this decision for several days if God does not reveal someone quickly.)

My spiritual director will be:

Prayer Posture:

STAND WITH HANDS LIFTED HIGH

Prayer Focus:

MY FRIENDS

_____

_____

_____

_____

_____

_____

_____

_____

_____

Day 74   Date: _____

Time: _____ Place: _____

Today's Passage:
1 JOHN 3:14-17

OBSERVE :: HEAD

Study Section:

What are the key words, phrases, and
ideas I see in this passage?

_____

_____

_____

_____

_____

_____

_____

_____

_____

_____

_____

INTERNALIZE :: HEART

Reflection Section:

How will this passage change the way I think and feel?

_____

_____

_____

_____

_____

_____

_____

EXTERNALIZE :: HANDS

Application Section:

How will this passage change the way I live?

_____

_____

_____

_____

_____

_____

_____

Key Verse from today:

Guidance

Refer back to the list of 5 things you feel the Lord is calling you to do (from Day 71).

Share that list with 3 close family members or friends in your life, and ask for their spiritual advice and guidance.

What was their response?
Share below.

Prayer Posture:

FIX YOUR GAZE ON HEAVEN & IMAGINE
STANDING AT THE THRONE OF GRACE

Prayer Focus:

MY CURRENT CIRCUMSTANCES & TRIALS

_____

_____

_____

_____

_____

_____

_____

_____

_____

Day 75   Date: _____

Time: _____   Place: _____

Today's Passage:
1 JOHN 3:18-24

OBSERVE :: HEAD

Study Section:

What are the key words, phrases, and
ideas I see in this passage?

_____

_____

_____

_____

_____

_____

_____

_____

_____

_____

INTERNALIZE :: HEART

Reflection Section:

How will this passage change the way I think and feel?

_____

_____

_____

_____

_____

_____

_____

_____

EXTERNALIZE :: HANDS

Application Section:

How will this passage change the way I live?

_____

_____

_____

_____

_____

_____

_____

Key Verse from today:

Guidance

Time to review your journal, as we seek God's guidance.

Take a highlighter, read through the last 11 weeks of your journal, look for the continual themes you find throughout.

Has God been speaking to something specific in your life through the last several weeks? Is there a repetitive truth? A constant prayer?

What did you find as you reviewed your journal?
Share below.

Prayer Posture:

5 MINUTE PRAYER WALK

Prayer Focus:

MY GOALS, DREAMS, & DESIRES

_____

_____

_____

_____

_____

_____

_____

_____

_____

_____

Day 76   Date: _____

Time: _____   Place: _____

Today's Passage:
REREAD 1 JOHN 3

OBSERVE :: HEAD

Study Section:

Did you see anything new as you read
through the chapter for a 2nd time?

_____

_____

_____

_____

_____

_____

_____

_____

_____

<u>INTERNALIZE :: HEART</u>

Reflection Section:

How will this passage change the way I
think and feel?

_____

_____

_____

_____

_____

_____

_____

_____

EXTERNALIZE :: HANDS

Application Section:

How will this passage change the way I live?

_____

_____

_____

_____

_____

_____

_____

Key Verse from today:

Guidance

Make the conscious effort as you interact with people today to listen for promptings from the Holy Spirit.

Ask God throughout the day to change your senses to make them more in tune with His Spirit.

May your eyes be open to see God's people.
May your ears be open to hear His voice.
May your hands be ready to serve, comfort, and offer a healing touch.
May your tongue be ready to taste, see, and share the goodness of God through encouraging Word and Truth.

Share your experience below.

Prayer Posture:

SIT IN SILENCE & LISTEN TO GOD FOR 5
MINUTES

Prayer Focus:

THE SALVATION OF SOMEONE WHO IS
LOST

_____

_____

_____

_____

_____

_____

_____

_____

_____

Day 77   Date: _____

Time: _____ Place: _____

Choose 1 verse to memorize from
1 JOHN 3

I will memorize...

Prayer Posture:
KNEELING WHILE PRAYING OUT LOUD

_____

_____

_____

_____

How did this week's focus on Guidance make you more spiritually mindful? Reflect on the quote below.

"One reason why we fail to hear God speak is that we are not attentive. We suffer from what might be called 'spiritual mindlessness.'"
– John Ortberg

This week, our spiritual discipline is the Discipline of Evangelism.

Some Christians have made the mistake of viewing evangelism as a spiritual gift only given to a few, rather than recognizing evangelism as a spiritual discipline that we all have the responsibility to practice. Yes, some might be called to be pastors and teachers, but we are ALL called to share the Gospel of Jesus Christ and make disciples.

Viewing evangelism as a discipline, as well as a delight, means that we sometimes choose to be with lost people in hopes of talking about Jesus with them.

And let's not forget that the gospel is a message we communicate through words - words about the person and work of Jesus Christ.

The Discipline of Evangelism is about intentionally speaking those words. While the consistency of our Christian example may affect the integrity of our witness, merely watching an example saves no one. Ultimately, it's not actions - important as they are - but the words of the "the gospel [that] is the power of God for salvation to everyone who believes" (Romans 1:16).

(The Gospel and the Discipline of Evangelism - https://www.lifeway.com/en/articles/spiritual-disciplines-gospel-evangelism-witnessing-missions-salvation-sharing-faith)

"Therefore go and make disciples of all nations, baptizing them in the name of the Father and of the Son and of the Holy Spirit, and teaching them to obey everything I have commanded you. And surely I am with you always, to the very end of the age." (Matthew 28:19-20)

Scripture Focus:
1 JOHN 4

Spiritual Disciplines:

BIBLE STUDY
PRAYER
FASTING
WORSHIP
MEDITATION
SILENCE + SOLITUDE
SIMPLICITY
SURRENDER
SERVICE
CONFESSION
GUIDANCE
& EVANGELISM

Dear FRIENDS, let us continue to LOVE one ANOTHER for love comes FROM God. ANYONE who LOVES is a CHILD of GOD and KNOWS God. 1 JOHN 4:7 ♡

Day 78   Date: _____

Time: _____ Place: _____

Today's Passage:
1 JOHN 4:1-3

OBSERVE :: HEAD

Study Section:

What are the key words, phrases, and
ideas I see in this passage?

_____

_____

_____

_____

_____

_____

_____

_____

_____

INTERNALIZE :: HEART

Reflection Section:

How will this passage change the way I
think and feel?

_____

_____

_____

_____

_____

_____

_____

_____

EXTERNALIZE :: HANDS

Application Section:

How will this passage change the way I live?

_____

_____

_____

_____

_____

_____

_____

Key Verse from today:

Evangelize

One of the most effective ways of sharing the Gospel is by sharing your personal story of Christ's work in your life.

"This same Good News that came to you is going out all over the world. It is bearing fruit everywhere by changing lives, just as it changed your lives from the day you first heard and understood the truth about God's wonderful grace."
(Colossians 1:6)

Take time to write out your testimony of salvation and how the Good News changed your life.

This is my story...

Prayer Posture:

KNEEL WITH HANDS OPEN TO HEAVEN

Prayer Focus:

MY COMMUNITY,
NATION, AND WORLD

_____

_____

_____

_____

_____

_____

_____

_____

_____

Day 79   Date: _____

Time: _____ Place: _____

Today's Passage
I JOHN 4:4-6

OBSERVE :: HEAD

Study Section:

What are the key words, phrases, and
ideas I see in this passage?

_____

_____

_____

_____

_____

_____

_____

_____

_____

_____

INTERNALIZE :: HEART

Reflection Section:

How will this passage change the way I
think and feel?

_____

_____

_____

_____

_____

_____

_____

_____

_____

EXTERNALIZE :: HANDS

Application Section:

How will this passage change the way I live?

Key Verse from today:

Evangelize

Pray and ask God to lay 2 people on your heart that you need to share the Gospel with this week.

Write down their names below.

I will share the Gospel with...

1.

2.

Prayer Posture:
STAND WITH HANDS LIFTED HIGH

Prayer Focus:
MY FAMILY

_____

_____

_____

_____

_____

_____

_____

_____

_____

_____

_____

Day 80   Date: _____

Time: _____ Place: _____

Today's Passage:
1 JOHN 4:7-10

OBSERVE :: HEAD

Study Section:

What are the key words, phrases, and
ideas I see in this passage?

_____

_____

_____

_____

_____

_____

_____

_____

_____

<u>INTERNALIZE :: HEART</u>

<u>Reflection Section:</u>

How will this passage change the way I think and feel?

_____

_____

_____

_____

_____

_____

_____

_____

_____

EXTERNALIZE :: HANDS

Application Section:

How will this passage change the way I
live?

_____

_____

_____

_____

_____

_____

_____

Key Verse from today:

Evangelize

What are the top 5 reasons you
hesitate sharing the Gospel?

Share below.

1.

2.

3.

4.

5.

Prayer Posture:

PRAY WHILE LYING PROSTRATE ON THE
FLOOR

Prayer Focus:

MY FRIENDS

_____

_____

_____

_____

_____

_____

_____

_____

_____

_____

Day 81   Date: _____

Time: _____ Place: _____

Today's Passage
1 JOHN 4:11-15

OBSERVE :: HEAD

Study Section:

What are the key words, phrases, and
ideas I see in this passage?

_____

_____

_____

_____

_____

_____

_____

_____

_____

_____

INTERNALIZE :: HEART

Reflection Section:

How will this passage change the way I
think and feel?

_____

_____

_____

_____

_____

_____

_____

EXTERNALIZE :: HANDS

Application Section:

How will this passage change the way I live?

_____

_____

_____

_____

_____

_____

_____

Key Verse from today:

Evangelize

Yesterday, you wrote down the top 5 reasons you hesitate sharing the Gospel.

Today, write down the top 5 reasons you are compelled to share the Gospel.

1.

2.

3.

4.

5.

Prayer Posture:
5 MINUTE PRAYER WALK

Prayer Focus:
MY CURRENT CIRCUMSTANCES & TRIALS

_____

_____

_____

_____

_____

_____

_____

_____

_____

_____

Day 82   Date: _____

Time _____ Place _____

Today's Passage:
1 JOHN 4:16-21

OBSERVE :: HEAD

Study Section:
What are the key words, phrases, and
ideas I see in this passage?

_____

_____

_____

_____

_____

_____

_____

_____

_____

_____

INTERNALIZE :: HEART

Reflection Section:

How will this passage change the way I think and feel?

_____

_____

_____

_____

_____

_____

_____

_____

_____

EXTERNALIZE :: HANDS

Application Section:

How will this passage change the way I live?

_____

_____

_____

_____

_____

_____

_____

_____

Key Verse from today:

Evangelize

Have you shared the Gospel with the 2 people God placed on your heart?

Why or why not?

If you have shared the Gospel with them, share your experience below.

If you have not, share what's holding you back.

Prayer Posture:

FIX YOUR GAZE ON HEAVEN & IMAGINE
STANDING AT THE THRONE OF GRACE

Prayer Focus:

MY GOALS, DREAMS, & DESIRES

_____

_____

_____

_____

_____

_____

_____

_____

_____

_____

Day 83   Date: _____

Time: _____ Place: _____

Today's Passage
REREAD 1 JOHN 4

<u>OBSERVE :: HEAD</u>

Study Section:

Did you see anything new as you read
through the chapter for a 2nd time?

_____

_____

_____

_____

_____

_____

_____

_____

_____

_____

INTERNALIZE :: HEART

Reflection Section:

How will this passage change the way I
think and feel?

_____

_____

_____

_____

_____

_____

_____

_____

_____

EXTERNALIZE :: HANDS

Application Section:

How will this passage change the way I live?

_____

_____

_____

_____

_____

_____

_____

Key Verse from today:

Evangelize

Pray and ask God to lay someone new on your heart to share the Gospel with.

Instead of a conversation, share the Gospel through a written letter to this person. Be sure to hand-deliver or mail the letter TODAY.

Share your experience below.

Prayer Posture:

SIT IN SILENCE & LISTEN TO GOD FOR 5 MINUTES

Prayer Focus:

THE SALVATION OF SOMEONE WHO IS LOST

_____

_____

_____

_____

_____

_____

_____

_____

_____

Day 84   Date: _____

Time: _____ Place: _____

Choose 1 verse to memorize from
1 JOHN 4

I will memorize...

Prayer Posture:
KNEELING WHILE PRAYING OUT LOUD

_____

_____

_____

_____

_____

_____

What was it like to consciously look
for opportunities to share the Gospel
this week?

Our last spiritual discipline is the Discipline of Celebration!

"Celebration brings joy into life, and joy makes us strong. Celebration is central to all the Spiritual Disciplines. Without a joyful spirit of festivity the Disciplines become dull, death-breathing tools in the hands of Modern Pharisees."
– Richard Foster

In many ways, joy is the motor of our spiritual life, and the Spiritual Discipline of Celebration fosters that joy. Joy is a fruit of the Holy Spirit, and that fruit is experienced by submission and obedience to the Holy Spirit.

We cannot experience the joy of the Lord, without choosing to walk in obedience and allow God to break into the common and routine parts of our every day lives.

Celebration is the means by which we invite God into our daily living, asking Him to redeem, revive, and restore the monotony of daily life.

Scripture Focus:

1 JOHN 5

Spiritual Disciplines:

BIBLE STUDY
PRAYER
FASTING
WORSHIP
MEDITATION
SILENCE + SOLITUDE
SIMPLICITY
SURRENDER
SERVICE
CONFESSION
GUIDANCE
EVANGELISM
& CELEBRATION

AND THIS IS
the confidence
THAT WE HAVE
toward him,
THAT IF WE
ASK ACCORDING
to his will
HE HEARS US.
first john
5:14

Day 85   Date: _____

Time: _____ Place: _____

Today's Passage:
I JOHN 5:1-5

OBSERVE :: HEAD

Study Section:

What are the key words, phrases, and
ideas I see in this passage?

_____

_____

_____

_____

_____

_____

_____

_____

_____

INTERNALIZE :: HEART

Reflection Section:

How will this passage change the way I
think and feel?

_____

_____

_____

_____

_____

_____

_____

_____

EXTERNALIZE :: HANDS

Application Section:

How will this passage change the way I live?

_____

_____

_____

_____

_____

_____

_____

Key Verse from today:

Celebrate

"The Christian should be an alleluia from head to foot!"
– Augustine of Hippo

The spirit of celebration often has to break through the hardened layer of the monotony, difficulty, and exhaustion of daily life.
Today, choose praise and gratitude over grumbling and complaining.
Write down 5 things you're grateful for:

1.

2.

3.

4.

5.

Prayer Posture:

PRAY WHILE LYING PROSTRATE ON THE
FLOOR

Prayer Focus:

MY COMMUNITY,
NATION, AND WORLD

_____

_____

_____

_____

_____

_____

_____

_____

_____

_____

Day 86   Date: _____

Time: _____ Place: _____

Today's Passage:
1 JOHN 5:6-12

OBSERVE :: HEAD

Study Section:

What are the key words, phrases, and ideas I see in this passage?

_____

_____

_____

_____

_____

_____

_____

_____

_____

INTERNALIZE :: HEART

Reflection Section:

How will this passage change the way I think and feel?

_____

_____

_____

_____

_____

_____

_____

_____

EXTERNALIZE :: HANDS

Application Section:

How will this passage change the way I live?

_____

_____

_____

_____

_____

_____

_____

_____

Key Verse from today:

Celebrate

"Then our mouth was filled with laughter, and our tongue with shouts of joy; then they said among the nations, 'The Lord has done great things for them.'"
(Psalm 126:2)

Choose laughter today. Even if you don't feel like it. Force yourself to smile. Look for reasons to laugh at yourself. Enjoy life and look for moments to laugh throughout your entire day.

Share your experience below.

Prayer Posture:

STAND WITH HANDS LIFTED HIGH

Prayer Focus:

MY FAMILY

_____

_____

_____

_____

_____

_____

_____

_____

_____

_____

_____

Day 87   Date: _____

Time: _____ Place: _____

Today's Passage:
1 JOHN 5:13-17

OBSERVE :: HEAD

Study Section:

What are the key words, phrases, and ideas I see in this passage?

_____

_____

_____

_____

_____

_____

_____

_____

_____

_____

INTERNALIZE :: HEART

Reflection Section:

How will this passage change the way I
think and feel?

_____

_____

_____

_____

_____

_____

_____

_____

_____

EXTERNALIZE :: HANDS

Application Section:

How will this passage change the way I
live?

_____

_____

_____

_____

_____

_____

_____

Key Verse from today:

Celebrate

Plan a celebration of sorts today. Find a reason to celebrate.

Here are some ideas:
Choose someone in your family to praise and have a special dinner honoring them.
Think of an event or accomplishment, and throw a party in celebration.

I'm sure you can come up with something! Share your idea below.

Prayer Posture:
KNEEL WITH HANDS OPEN TO HEAVEN

Prayer Focus:
MY FRIENDS

_____

_____

_____

_____

_____

_____

_____

_____

_____

_____

_____

Day 88   Date: _____

Time: _____ Place: _____

OBSERVE :: HEAD

Study Section:

What are the key words, phrases, and
ideas I see in this passage?

_____

_____

_____

_____

_____

_____

_____

_____

_____

_____

_____

INTERNALIZE :: HEART

Reflection Section:

How will this passage change the way I
think and feel?

_____

_____

_____

_____

_____

_____

_____

EXTERNALIZE :: HANDS

Application Section:

How will this passage change the way I live?

_____

_____

_____

_____

_____

_____

_____

Key Verse from today:

Celebrate

"Joy is a spiritual discipline. We as a people are much more inclined toward negativity and cynicism. We don't find it easy or natural to pursue joy. And that's why God in His Word actually commands us to celebrate. We come by a Gospel worth celebrating before a celebrating king. We need to get down to the serious business of joy. We must wrestle for our blessing. We must fight for our joy."
- Gareth Gilkeson

What negativity or cynicism in life keeps you from celebrating? Share below.

Prayer Posture:

5 MINUTE PRAYER WALK

Prayer Focus:

MY CURRENT CIRCUMSTANCES & TRIALS

_____

_____

_____

_____

_____

_____

_____

_____

_____

_____

Day 89   Date: _____

Time: _____ Place: _____

Today's Passage:
REREAD 1 JOHN 5

OBSERVE :: HEAD

Study Section:
What are the key words, phrases, and
ideas I see in this passage?

_____

_____

_____

_____

_____

_____

_____

_____

_____

INTERNALIZE :: HEART

Reflection Section:

How will this passage change the way I
think and feel?

_____

_____

_____

_____

_____

_____

_____

_____

_____

EXTERNALIZE :: HANDS

Application Section:

How will this passage change the way I live?

_____

_____

_____

_____

_____

_____

_____

Key Verse from today:

Celebrate

Throughout Scripture, God set up festivals, so that the people of God would celebrate and remember God's grace in their lives.

Be creative and plan a way to celebrate all that God has done in your life.

Share about your celebration below.

Prayer Posture:

FIX YOUR GAZE ON HEAVEN & IMAGINE
STANDING AT THE THRONE OF GRACE

Prayer Focus:

MY GOALS, DREAMS, & DESIRES

_____

_____

_____

_____

_____

_____

_____

_____

_____

_____

Day 90   Date: _____

Time: _____ Place: _____

Choose 1 verse to memorize from
1 JOHN 5

I will memorize...

Prayer Posture:
KNEELING WHILE PRAYING OUT LOUD

Prayer Focus:
RECENT ANSWERED PRAYERS

_____

_____

_____

_____

_____

_____

_____

_____

_____

_____

_____

_____

As we bring this 90-day journey to a close, take a moment to celebrate and reflect on all God has taught you over the last 13 weeks.
What are your major takeaways?
Share below.

_____

_____

_____

_____

_____

_____

_____

_____

_____

50499515R00251

Made in the USA
Columbia, SC
10 February 2019